Summer

A DUBAI MEMOIR

BUSOLA OKEWUMI

These events are my memories from my
perspective. Certain names have been changed
to protect the identities of those involved.

The scriptures quoted are taken from the Holy
Bible, "New International Version" (NIV)
Unless otherwise indicated.

NIV Giant Print Reference Bible

Copyright © 2011 by Zondervan

The New International Version (NIV) text may
be quoted in any form (written, visual,
electronic, or audio), up to and inclusive of five

ISBN-13:

9798783069727

Cover design by Lusions Interactive Digital

Agency +234 806 468 1664

Summer is coming

In honor of Victoria and Olu Okewumi, who both meant everything and gave all the love that any child will need.

CONTENTS

Summer Is Coming

Summer Is Coming

SUMMER IS COMING

"My theory on life is that life is beautiful. Life doesn't change. You have a day, and a night, and a month, and a year. We people change - we can be miserable, or we can be happy. It's what you make of your life."

Mohammed Bin Rashid Al Maktoum

I was disconcerted when I first heard it. "We must book our tickets, pack the kids' bags, and, of course, freeze all memberships."

I had overheard a baritone voice in the parking lot. Her voice was extremely husky and loud that I thought it was a man until I saw her up close in female activewear as she hurriedly threw her shopping bags and yoga props in the trunk of a white Mazda CX-5 and rushed in. I looked around to see why she seemed to be in a hurry because it now suddenly looked like the other few people in the parking lot were in a hurry too. Within minutes, it dawned on me.

Unlike House Stark in Game of Thrones when winter approaches, the opposite is unarguably the case in this part of the world. Every summer, it is normal for people to escape for as long as they can with everywhere becoming quieter except for tourists who roam around.

I blamed Uncle Yup several times for my decision to move outside my homeland. He had made living abroad seem like luxury all year round, so I never imagined the worst.

Whenever Uncle Yup returned from America, his talks were filled with "Yup," "I know," and "You know" even in sentences that did not need them - so much that my parents started to call him "yup yup."

The way he spoke English with a loud voice and so much confidence as if he needed our neighbors to hear him intentionally, often annoyed my mum. His accent was also quite different from what I heard on T-V, so, I used to laugh: I thought he tried too hard.

Everyone always gathered around him especially because of the dozens of antiperspirants he bought as gifts from "the abroad." His mannerisms amused me more than I was interested in his gifts. His shoulders were always high to his chin whenever he walked, and he would demonstrate everything he said with his hands as though there was an imaginary deaf person around. He made me desire to live abroad. There is something about a Nigerian man living abroad. He automatically becomes more important in the family. Like a mini-god.

Whether my uncle was being fake or real, I knew that I wanted the kind of aura he had. That aura I could only get living anywhere else apart from my country of birth. I desired that knowledgeable and confidence-reeking aura that came from his stories so much that I would stand in front of my mirror and mimic him.

After years of desiring to move, I finally made up my mind - or more like, I was fed up and forced out of my own beloved country by a desire for something different, so I moved to the United Arab Emirates, which is only about seven hours of flying from Lagos. I should have gone to America where my uncle lived but it was easier for me to go to the UAE, or it may have just been what my pastor calls 'destiny' that played out.

Whatever the case at the time, I did not care because something new and different was calling out to me and it was from a far country. I prepared myself in all ways possible and was as ready as a desperate soul except I was not ready for one major thing. The sun.

Or better still, Summer.

No one ever really mentioned that part to me. They all just talked about how beautiful it was in Dubai and their level of security. Those were my top reasons for settling for the city. I may have stumbled on an article that I probably read in passing when I researched the weather conditions and I must have thought, "The sun shines everywhere. Not a big deal."

Truth is, I never really understood the Celsius and

Fahrenheit brouhaha enough to bother about it because I grew up knowing just rainy and dry seasons. I saw winter only in movies and I pretty much knew what sunshine was, only that I never knew there was a different type of sunshine that hides at night but still flexes its powers around the 40 degrees mark.

I had always imagined living abroad, but the fear of being away from family as the last child killed my thoughts most of the time. Even though my mum would not let me out of her sight for too long, she fueled my imagination with her words.

Whenever my hair was styled in a ponytail, "You look like an American babe", she used to say, and I always smiled, and cat walked as though that was how Americans walked. She was my hype woman and I loved her for that.

The kind of summer that happens in Dubai should be given an entirely different name. The word 'Summer' does not really accord it the exact meaning. There's 'Summer' and then there is 'Dubai Summer'. Unrivaled. Imagine walking in an open-air sauna every day.

The only summer vacation you really do not need but still go on anyway because it is Dubai, and you end up lamenting about the high humidity the entire time, but it still does not stop you from shopping and finding all the places you had seen online before travelling. Many tourists do not even know that Dubai residents flee the city for cooler climates during summer. Thank God for air conditioners and uninterrupted power supply, those of us who stay back in summer can get by. So, I do not blame the lady with the baritone voice anyway, she probably lived most of her life in a cooler climate before moving to Dubai with her ex-pat husband and children but just cannot stand six long months of round the clock heat.

As with other seasons, the hope of summer is the mental picture that the word projects to our minds. For many, summer automatically means happiness and fun. However, until I arrived in Dubai, I never realized it is not always fun and happiness for everyone. Some people need to be extra intentional about the results they will get in the summertime.

Summer is whatever you make of it, so do what you must to make it an enjoyable season even if it means fleeing. If I could also afford to get away for as long as I wanted, I will never have had to deal with self-acclaimed dermatologists that made me go broke from buying skin care products.

HABIBTI, YOU'RE NOT ALONE

More than anything, my wish for you is this: That when your awful darkest days come, you will know you're not alone. Pain will tell you to keep quiet, but that's a lie. Life is fragile and we all break in different ways. I hope you know you can be honest. I hope you know that you can ask for help. Did you catch that? It is absolutely positively okay to ask for help. It simply means you're human. Help is real and it is possible; people find it every day."

Jamie Tworkowski

Surviving an accident that tattooed massive scars on specific parts of my body at the age of eight did not quite help with my confidence for a very long time. I did not understand it until about four years later in prep school. I had returned to boarding school for what my school termed 'Extension'. These extended classes were organized for juniors and seniors preparing for the standard test administered by the West African Examinations Council (WAEC). Upon successful completion of the examination, juniors graduate to senior school while seniors graduate to study in their university of choice.

Everyone looked forward to extension classes, but I honestly preferred to be home, studying on my own or with the help of a tutor because prep time sucked the energy out of me. I was always easily distracted by every movement and had difficulty concentrating in forced silence.

Each reading table was set up in such a way that one might never see a familiar face, and I used to sit there wondering if everyone was really studying. I just was never able to focus. It distracted me and, many times, I dozed off till the next sound disturbed my sleep.

That day, I did not wear my hostel uniform because we were few in the class, so I sort of had the liberty to focus on my reading - until I heard a senior behind me whisper loudly, "Eww!"

I turned. She and another senior were gaping at my shoulder. I had never imagined that I would be an object of disgust to anyone in my lifetime, so I was shocked. I looked back at my notebook and pretended I did not just see two people gawk at the scar on my shoulder. I was mortified and hoped no one else would join in their horror.

I could not help but remember the horrific accident that rendered me unconscious for a day; the excruciating pain from the multiple injuries on the right side of my face, shoulder, and legs; as well as the constant "What happened to you?" questions I had to answer. I wondered what they would say if the wound on my face had not healed with faint scarring.

Thankfully, my sister who was also a senior in my school happened to be present in the prep class, so I wrote a note about what had just happened and how I felt and passed it across to her table. Writing about how I felt may have helped me get over it that day, but I never wore clothes that revealed my scars anymore. That was where my body insecurities began and boy, did it grow.

***

"Hello, my name is Reem, what about you?"

"My name is Busola."

"Oh, nice name, Busola means compass in my language. Do you know that?" Reem asked smiling.

"Really? I never knew that. The full name is Oluwabusola and that translates to 'God has added to my wealth'. This would mean that when my parents conceived me, they had major financial blessings. Instead of naming me 'Blessing' as most parents would, I got a name that translates into a sentence – Oluwabusola. My other names as well as my last name also translate into sentences in English. Many people who are born in my part of the world are named this way." I smiled.

"So Reem, I have varying tones of exotic brown on my skin." I continued after she asked me what my major skin concerns were.

I had met Reem during one of my fun window shopping in the Mall of the Emirates. There was a beauty store that had an ongoing sale, and after the sales representative had cajoled me in, she directed me to Reem, their in-store dermatologist who offered me a free consultation at my convenience. She made me feel very comfortable and so I divulged relevant and irrelevant information about myself and my skin to her.

"I have an uneven skin tone. My face is not black, but it is a few shades darker than the rest of my body, but not all the time". She looked like I had confused her.

"Sometimes it is brown, most times it is coffee brown, and other times it is slightly caramel. If you look closely, you will notice the chiaroscuro technique on this beautiful brown skin - going from coffee brown to chocolate and then some caramel too." I showed her by pointing at different angles on my left hand.

"If you asked me, I'll say I am an excellent work of art, but some people do not think the same way especially after I moved to Dubai."

She kept looking at me with keen interest as I gave her a

mini show.

I continued, telling her how one would think that it is only when living in a multicultural environment that you start noticing how different one's skin color is. However, this comparison is ridiculously an unbelievable practice among black people because of the different shades of dark skin tones that exist.

As I spoke, her phone beeped, and we both looked at it. She ignored the call and I continued again.

"I have had friends who told me to bleach or lighten my face to match the rest of my body. I have been in relationships where I was constantly asked if I had been out working in the sun."

I spoke to her passionately explaining how producing melanin in the sun is a defense mechanism for the skin, as opposed to all the fallacies around it - as if she did not know.

I told her about how I often got criticized about my uneven skin tone - It just never feels okay for a human to have an uneven skin tone like mine. So, when we see dark knuckles or dark patches, we start to recommend all kinds of acids that we see on the internet: "Have you tried this goat milk?" "You should try using this serum" and many other suggestions - all without carefully asking the right questions. It may just be that a person with dark knuckles needs to start wearing rubber gloves to handwash their dishes and delicate clothes instead of using bare hands.

I had spoken at length and knew I should stop talking, but the more I talked to her, the more I saw a need to just let it all out.

"As soon as I started to experience hyperpigmentation, a new level of insecurity began for me. I invested heavily in creams, toners, cleansers, serums, boosters, oils of all kinds, black soaps. Guess what? The products worked, but they did not stop me from producing melanin. They only helped to hide it to an extent. I needed to consistently buy more products, so whenever I am broke, my skin suffers."

"I understand how you feel…," she tried to interrupt me, but I cut her.

"I have seen a couple of dermatologists and I must say that that was the beginning of a financial episode of my life when I simply started to say 'money is to be spent anyways', just to feel justified. I eventually stopped trying to fix it and embraced all my beautiful shades of black – and brown. I discovered that producing more melanin on my face than other parts of my body was normal as I started to study my own body personally. I realized that it had more to do with my cycle, eating habits, and the effects of these on my hormones."

On the other hand, Google's diagnoses nearly drove me *noncompos mentis*. Who vets all the research that gets posted on Google for goodness' sake?!

"Studies on Google however show that melanin protects us from skin cancer. Another theory states that melanin can also do us harm. So Reem, is melanin protecting me and causing my skin damage at the same time, is producing melanin harmful to me?"

At this point I was exhausted, so I took a deep breath and rolled my eyes. I had finally stopped talking. Looking straight into Reem's eyes, she looked like she was wondering if I needed a skin consultation or mental therapy during my session - and then she laughed so hard, she started to cough.

"I'll advise you avoid sun exposure between 10 a.m. and

3 p.m."

She managed to speak between laughter and was about recommending a mineral sunscreen for my sensitive skin when I dramatically interrupted her again.

"Fair enough Reem, I'm at work or home between those hours every day. However, it is that moment I go out to take a delivery package or walk into the grocery store across the road, those five minutes in the sun, that mess everything up." I looked at her, hoping she understood my point.

"These sunscreens are a waste because I don't think they do the job. If I buy a 30 SPF sunscreen and I am at work, does it not mean that I have to reapply that every three hours, in between meetings and work?!"

"I nearly choked on my laughter, sweetheart. You have a beautiful black skin. See her as your most precious gift and just continue to care for her because that's what you do with a gift. Consistency is the magic Habibti, you are not alone".

"Nah, Reem. Money is the magic." I rolled my eyes and we both laughed but her profound words stuck.

"Busola" she pronounced the Bu in my name as boo and the sola as solar.

"Habibti, carry an umbrella or wear a nice hat whenever you're in the sun. Then use a gentle cleanser on your face at night and in the morning, apply the sunscreen you have after cleansing. Do this consistently for a month, then come back to me after, okay?" She picked up a very affordable hydrating cleanser and gave me a discount on it.

None of my self-acclaimed dermatologists had been that helpful in the past. The first one offered me full coverage makeup options. I later found out she was a make-up artist that sold make-up on the side. Ugh!

The second one just clearly wanted to sell high-end products from her drug store so she recommended cleansers that cost a fortune. Everyone, it seems, is just technically out to satisfy their pockets - and not make an impactful difference in lives.

Kai, my light-skinned Ghanaian dermatologist who I met at my friend's wedding, was ready to take me through a microdermabrasion process, but I had to leave town for a few weeks at the time, so, she recommended a consistent Vitamin C diet. For some weird reason, my melanin production increased dramatically as I possibly overdosed on Vitamin C. The silver lining here was that my immune system became stronger. It was all just a confusing situation, so I decided to let it all go and let myself breathe - knowing full well that I had done my best.

Before I met Reem, I had gotten used to buying two shades of foundation because I never found my exact shade: a medium shade, and a dark shade just so that when I blend, it will give me what I need - and truly, this helped me a great deal. However, when people say things like "You look so beautiful," I always wondered why those kinds of compliments were only passed when my layers of foundation were on. So, for a long time, I could not be caught outside my home without at least some elements of makeup on.

Reem did not try to fix my melanin issues, nor did she try to even out my skin tone, but she helped me embrace a minimalist approach to taking care of my skin to a point where my insecurities shrunk, and I was finally able to do without make-up.

It might be difficult for people to accept you the way you look - or as you experience changes in your body -

which will happen from time to time, but somehow when you finally get yourself to that point of accepting yourself and the way you change, people will eventually align but ensure you speak your truth and ask for help whenever you feel overwhelmed with people's expectations of you and what you should look like.

Habibti, you are not alone.

EMIRATI MEN ARE BEAUTIFUL

That's the problem with beautiful men. They don't know their impact; they don't realize how a casually tossed out thought can be devoured, obsessed over, life-changing".

Alessandra Torre

There was something about the air on Sheikh Zayed road that seemed so different when I first rode through with an open sunroof from the airport. It blew contrary to what I was used to and felt less gentle on the skin - not like the air we called "fresh" back home. It felt rather sweltering and was at the same time condensed, as though there were too many invisible obstructions in the air, making it almost airless.

If the leaves on the trees had not been moving, I would have said there was no air at all. Even the leaves did not move like normal leaves. They looked like they moved forcefully because they froze more than they moved, or maybe it had something to do with that time of the year. It was early October and winter was not yet in full effect. Perhaps the effect of air from the fast-moving cars made the leaves move from time to time.

The random cars driving by were very few. Everyone seemed to be living the good life in this city. It felt like the road itself was a huge showroom where people were either test driving or showing off.

It did not feel real until after a couple more days when I started getting used to it. "People drive actual

Lamborghinis, Ferraris, and G-Wagons to work every day?" I would think to myself each time I saw luxury cars parked in front of any building. "What is this place, dear Lord? Some bougie desert where you decided to keep the flashy things of life?"

I worried God a lot with all my rhetorical questions.

I was told people do not drive responsibly in Dubai, but from what I saw in my first few hours from the airport, it was obvious they were a hundred times better than some people I know. I could barely hear honking sounds, and no one was stopping by the roadside of an expressway just to say hello to a fellow driver friend they had stumbled on in traffic. They were doing an amazing job behind the wheels - or maybe I just was not used to law and order to notice their bad driving.

As we drove to what would be my new home for the next month, I saw dunes of white sand and wondered why our sand back home had to be brownish. "Maybe it has something to do with the color of our skin," I thought. There were vast empty lands with absolutely nothing on them but white sand.

I could not help but think about how every piece of

land is already owned by someone in Lagos, and their habit of covering the land with roof sheets and bold warnings of "THIS LAND IS NOT FOR SALE" which is rarely written correctly most of the time. The irony, however, is that the cited land, usually, has already been sold. However, just in case the powerful people who claim their father owns all lands ('ọmọ-onilẹs' as they are called) come around, the warning is supposed to give them an understanding.

I laughed at my thoughts as I soaked in the view of a beautifully maintained city.

Before we got home, we stopped to get me a few things at one of the major malls. I did not quite understand why the mall looked extremely beautiful. I had never seen a mall that was as carefully planned and designed - and, no, it was not the Dubai mall. This one is called Ibn Battuta Mall, named after the renowned scholar, Ibn Battuta. The mall features six different zones - India, China, Egypt, Persia, Tunisia, and Andalusia courts - each representing the culture and architecture of the countries Ibn famously explored.

I fell in love with this mall for many reasons and only shopped there for the next one year - one of the reasons being the fine Emirati men. I had seen an Emirati man up close in that mall for the first time and, boy, was he fine!

Emirati men are beautiful, especially the ones in uniform. Imagine a police officer walking up to you, and the first thing you do is smile and blink your eyes countless times - before you get handcuffed and realize that you are going to jail. That is exactly how pleasing they are to the eyes.

Their women are gorgeous too, in almost perfect body conditions, if you know what I mean. But I am not trying to tell you about the women now. Let us focus on the facial features of their men only.

On that very day, I wanted nothing more than to be a Nigerian Emirati. I nearly stumbled as I stared at this young man in his white Kandura and white slippers. He was nothing short of the word - clean, white never looked so spotless. I feared what my shade of foundation would do to the neck region of his dress as I imagined giving him a tight hug.

However, as much as I wanted to describe him as an angel, there was something about him that did not quite qualify for that angelic description: His face looked too sweet - I could lick him all up - and the way he kept running his right hand through his very black hair made my brain move back and forth for a few seconds. He was just standing there, watching as people moved about, and I wondered why he would just stand in the middle of a place and cause me that much heart and brain clog at the same time.

I later learned he was an undercover police officer - even better, as I yearned to see him in his real uniform. This was only because I had seen the immigration officers at the airport and thought, "Damn! These men are clean" but the tension at the immigration point did not give me the chance to appreciate them well.

Men in uniform should look super attractive. Their uniforms, gait, rigid discipline, and the danger they face every day are all elements of their personae that make them attractive. Psychologists believe that women gravitate towards men in uniform because they signify purpose and valor. That is how it should be - but there is something not so attractive about the "Men in Black" or "Men in orange" or "Men in blue" in my home country. I guess it has to do with the rank. The lower the rank, the uglier they look.

My Emirati boo finally walked towards me, and I almost froze. I became nervous as I felt a war starting in my belly. My intestines were suddenly tangled together like a confused Bantu knot as if to protect me from some unknown danger. I looked away for a minute just so I could look startled when he reached me. One, two, three minutes went by, and I was still looking away - only to hear some Arabic chatter a few meters away. I turned to see what was going on, and I saw him rubbing nose with another man dressed exactly alike with the sharpest sound of a kiss I had ever heard.

My eyeballs nearly popped out from their lids.

At that point, my friend returned from his mini shopping, and we had to head home. Images of a nose rub between two men did not leave my head. I wanted to ask my friend so bad, but I decided to keep it cool.

"It's got to have a meaning to it", I thought to myself.

As soon as I got home, Google was kind enough to answer my questions. It is a form of greeting that portrays a level of respect and friendship. It is known as an Eskimo kiss or better still, the 'Khashm-makh'. The pronunciation of this word is another struggle entirely as the 'k' is silent - just in case you want to try it out. This, however, was the beginning of my journey in the UAE.

LAMENTATIONS 101

If the sun said it had power over the moon, then let it come and shine

at night.

African Proverb

*W*hy did I choose to do this to myself?"

what made me think I could find it in this city?"

Why haven't I even found it yet?"

When will I possibly find it?"

These were the questions I kept asking myself each time I got out of the house, without being able to give a tangible answer; and as I walked to the roadside this day, I was not cat walking. I was walking haphazardly from shade to shade with the full-on hot flashes I was experiencing.

I squatted with my friend in a small developing area so there were very few things in sight and every corner looked similar. On my left was a dune that looked like an interrupted river flow that could not move to the road, and to my right were uncompleted high-rise buildings with continuous noise of construction work. The grocery store on the other side of the road was empty and I wondered if they made enough profit to even pay their employees monthly.

The sun was blazing relentlessly that Sunday afternoon, the air so thick one could break through it. It felt good for just a couple of minutes after coming out of a normal sixteen degrees. But the goodness soon delved into a monstrous attack that led me into a frenzy of anxiety. No one was out on the streets except the construction workers who probably had a terrific deadline to meet. I could only imagine how their blood must be boiling from the effects of the spherical celestial fireball in the sky.

I had never felt anything quite intense in my entire life and considering that we were many millions of kilometers away from the sun, I wanted a more fascinating reason for such high temperature and humidity - other than the fact that we were situated at the north of the equator. I am never really going to understand science because that is not enough reason.

I felt the UV-B rays hit my skin and, in a couple of minutes, the way my skin darkened made me believe in the effectiveness of the sun and its effortless result in a sunburn. Even though I was beginning to enjoy undiluted Vitamin D, I was afraid that I might have produced too much melanin for one day. If I could sell melanin to people desperate for tanned skin, I will be a billionaire by now.

I could feel my temperature rising by the minute, but thankfully, what does not kill you either makes you stronger or darker in my case.

The Sunna in the United Arab Emirates is forever shining unapologetically with the air as still as death in summer. I nearly went blind when I looked up as I waited for a taxi. This moment got me wondering what the Israelites must have gone through for a whopping forty years in the desert.

My makeup was melting slowly, and my true color was beginning to show physically and mentally. Little wonder why many residents 'elope' for months and return when the weather is slightly cooler. A high percentage of the people that remain in Dubai during the summer are tourists and, of course, those of us that cannot afford to be away for too long for varied reasons.

I could stay for a year, but I had planned to stay for just six months, and "I will only be staying that long." I said that to myself every day; but four years later I was still there, producing so much melanin in the summer.

After about thirty minutes of an unwanted sunbath, I finally saw a taxi approaching. As I quickly flagged it down, I noticed two ladies coming out from a shed, flagging down "my" taxi. As though I was now too dark to be seen, the taxi passed me by, made a U-turn, and stopped right in front of them. What just happened?! I yelled, jumped, and waved my right hand in the air to catch the driver's attention - I was so certain he saw me.

I pulled out my mirror angrily to see if I had an "ignore-me" sign on my face, but I only saw half my face with makeup and the other half with very high pigmentation. I wiped my face, infuriated, walked back to the apartment, and stayed indoors till I was able to manage the colors on my face to the barest minimum. Wherever I was headed was no longer as important as my wellbeing, thanks to the sun. I was told later that the taxi's decision not to stop for me was because of my skin color. So rude!

"I'm still trying to understand why you gave up that New York offer for this hot mess, Busola," Adeife rolled her eyes and shook her head as she spoke.

"Yeah, story of my life..." I rolled my own eyes for the umpteenth time. It was as if we were in an eye-rolling competition.

"I mean, I'm just tired of your constant nags. Maybe you should come back home."

25

"Jeez, enough already! Okay, I won't complain any more - can we please change the topic?"

Adey would not stop whining about how I had made the wrong choice. That was the only way she could tell me how much she missed me and how she wanted me back home. That was all I heard from her daily pep talks.

"Dubai is listed among places to go holidaying, not schooling! Anyways, I will drop it. So, tell me about that guy you're living with."

"Shut up Adey, walls have ears. I'll tell you how school is going instead."

"Boring girl. I have to go now, talk later."

The video call ended, and I was back to my reality. Adey was right: my life was indeed boring.

I was not sure whether it was my upbringing or the fact that it is against the law to cohabit with a man you are not married to that got me feeling bad for a long time. Even though the law has now been relaxed, I could only imagine my daughter living with a male friend to better understand the situation, and that was basically why I never discussed my life with anyone, not even Adey - at

26

least until I moved to my own apartment.

I often wondered what the case would be if it became a law all over the world to not cohabit with the opposite sex. We might end up having more same-sex couples than the world being a better place. How about a law that ensures everyone is good to their neighbors? Now, that seems a bit more realistic to me.

Living in a villa with five young men - mostly short guys, not exactly my type at the time - was very new to me. I had to condition my mind to think of them as my brothers. Growing up with more girls than guys made it difficult to adjust. A couple of them thought I was shy. I was truly shy, but I was also grieving, and my coping mechanism was to be alone. One of the guys even threatened to break down the door to the room because I was always locked up in the room. No one could understand why I enjoyed my own company so much. More like, why I loved boredom so much.

This was not the case back home: there, everyone would pretend to be asleep when I started to talk too much, or they would tell me to go help look for something that was not missing just so they could get some peace. My mum had once told me to go ask the neighbor for some strange thing called *àródan*. Our neighbor then told me they had given it to the neighbors on the other side. So, I went to ask them. After I had gone to the end of the street and back, knocking on every door and getting drained by the minute, I later found out that *àródan* was an approach to give a stressed mother a break by occupying the child.

***

After the call with Adey, I heard a motorcycle with its engine continuously revving at a high pitch from the terrace, and as I rushed out to see if it was my neighbor, I hit my left foot against the wooden leg of the bed frame. I dropped my entire weight on the bed, closed my eyes, and sighed heavily but softly because I did not want to disturb my quiet neighbors.

"Jesus, Jesus, help me. I can't afford any more pain this week. Please help me," I said groaning.

I attempted to get up quickly, but the pain would not let me. I tried again and sat back down, raising both legs and moving them from side to side. When I finally mustered a little strength to limp out to the balcony, I saw nothing. I sighed and went back in. Adey would have had a refreshing moment of breathless laughter if she had seen the way I hit my leg for nothing.

I love Adeife a lot, mainly because of her name which means "Crown of love." We met at the finishing school I attended after my one-year National youth service program in Lagos. We sat next to each other on the first day of class and became inseparable ever since.

Adey is extremely amiable and has a magical effect that makes people like her. Most times I think it is because of her skin color. There is just something about light-skinned ladies that draws people to them. It has nothing to do with their personality. So, when you meet a light-skinned lady with a good personality, it is like finding a big piece of gold inserted in a miniature gold piece.

I was drawn to Adey's versatility and ability to adapt to anything life throws her way. She had lost both parents a long time back but lives life with the mantra, "Impossible is nothing."

Adey is forever committing fashion crimes and still wears clothes from four years ago, as she has not gained any weight since we first met five years ago. She sometimes looks hot and most times not, but I am yet to understand why she has more male admirers than I do. Probably because she is very easy-going and looks more approachable than I do.

She is a sweetheart, but I just cannot tell her everything because she is an inexplicable chatterbox. She talks when she is tired, and I sometimes feel like she has a special separate energy source that supplies strength to her vocal cords and mouth directly from the universe.

For the next few days after that day, I stayed indoors and realized that the effect of the scorching sun is probably why nightlife is a big deal in Dubai.

LAGOS NIGERIA

…And hope does not put us to shame…

Romans 5:5 (NIV)

I was born and bred in a community called Ikotun in the megacity of Lagos. Èkó, as I like to call my favorite city in the world, is the most populated city in Nigeria. Oh, I bet you didn't know that." I said to Cruz, smiling with a raised neck and so much pride.

"Oh wow, so are you like one of those African princesses?" Cruz asked as he drove and tried to stay on a 120km speed limit on the fast lane.

My heart was racing faster than the car as I thought my story of Lagos fueled Cruz's excitement to drive faster in his GMC truck which had tires that were half my height and constantly screeched every time he turned or pressed on the brakes.

I tried to distract myself and continued with my story of Lagos. "Err, I...I like to think of myself as an African princess, but I wasn't born into any royal family."

"So, what's so special about Lagos?" Cruz took his eyes off the road for a moment, and I watched as he vroomed past the cars on other lanes. "Lagosians!" I shouted with much excitement. "Lagosians are the locals, just like the Emiratis. They make Lagos a world-class destination and set the city apart from other cities.

The vibe you get from them, the unnecessary anger, judgment, and careful love will make you enjoy every other thing better - the beaches, few skyscrapers, and amazing parks.

"Lagos has the best entertainment options, most job opportunities are in Lagos and, just like a lot of people move abroad searching for greener pastures, people have moved from other states in Nigeria to find jobs in Lagos over the years." I sighed deeply as we drove into a parking space in one of the largest malls in the world. I just could not imagine what the largest mall in the world would then be like.

Cruz is tall and was the only Caucasian out of the five guys that lived in the villa. I liked his golden beard, but its thickness was now like a dirty, old mop stick with yarns sticking out in all directions. The way his pointed nose rested on his narrow face made him look like a woodpecker that was always ready to tap into a tree trunk. This probably explains why he never minds his business. He had a different kind of British accent I had never heard before. I had thought that one of the other guys had influenced him with the Nigerian 'h' factor because sometimes, he dropped an 'h' between his words.

He would say "e" instead of "he" and then prolong the "r" even in sentences that do not have "r". He would say "Chelsea/r/ and Liverpool/r/ are playing." Most times, I would just nod my head or act like I did not hear a thing he said because I was tired of having to ask him to repeat himself.

How he was able to blend with four short, black guys never bothered me. I just liked his free spirit a lot.

He was going to be driving twenty-three kilometers from Jumeirah village circle to the very massive Dubai mall just to get a haircut and I had thought to tag along since I had not been there before.

He was nice enough to be my tour guide and bought me lunch after we searched tirelessly for the barbershop but soon found out that they had probably moved. Yes, he had forgotten the name of the shop - and where could we even start to find one shop out of a thousand and one shops in such a huge mall measuring in millions of square feet. It is as big as the whole of Dubai stacked together on five floors.

While we had lunch, I told him how the fries tasted nice

with the cheese but that I preferred my experience at a Lagos restaurant where I had tried fish and chips for the first time and thought it was heaven. I explained how the service was exceptional and, even though I had not been abroad before the time, I had felt like I was on Wall Street having the best lunch ever that day. I had spent just as much money as we were spending having lunch, and I had had a better view of nature - and amazing fresh air - than what I was experiencing at the Dubai Mall.

Cruz immediately Googled the restaurant and read their reviews online. I am not sure why he checked, but I guess he was unlearning the story of Africa that he had heard. I felt like a proud Lagosian who needed to put Lagos side by side Dubai every time I got asked a question about what it was like in Nigeria.

That did not even last for long because reality set in soon enough.

My heels got so numb from walking through every corner of the mall.

"Oh, my goodness! How come?" I looked up at Cruz who is about 6.5 feet with my eyes wide open like I had just seen my ex-boyfriend's face on his forehead.

"What's the matter? Are you okay?" He looked traumatized, and I could see how blood rushed into his face making him look red.

"Err it…. I…. it's 11:40 p.m." I said slowly, not sure I was supposed to have caused an alarm just because of what my wristwatch was telling me.

"Oh, I'm sorry, are you supposed to be somewhere by now?" Cruz asked, still trying to figure out what the exact issue was. I had to tell him I had missed an important family video call slated for 9 p.m. and how they would have been worried. The real reason, however, was that I had not been out so late before, and seeing the time took me aback for a moment.

That was the beginning of my reality – Dubai is not Lagos.

I had grown up living on an outskirt of Lagos, so, whenever I went out, I would leave for home by 6 p.m. at the latest to be home by 9 p.m.; and if there were unforeseen problems, I would sometimes get home not later than 10:30 p.m.

The day I went out partying with my friends at the

beach - a very meaningless party by the way - I almost peed in my pants from the anxiety of what punishments I would get for returning home at past midnight. My dad did not talk to me for days, and that meant I was grounded for the entire time it took him to get over it.

Cruz and I got home after midnight, and everyone was still awake and unbothered about the time. That was something I had to adjust to. Even though I was happy I now had endless freedom of time and no more curfews, the Ikotun girl in me still obeyed my father's curfews in faraway Dubai. This is the true example of the Yoruba saying, "Ranti ọmọ ẹ́ni ti iwọ n she." (Remember the child of whom you are).

-

A few weeks later, my face had finally gotten better, many thanks to all the YouTube channels I went on to get answers to a brighter and healthier look. I tried lemon, honey, turmeric, apple cider vinegar, and lots more. I was feeding my face with all sorts of food.

"There are so many channels on YouTube, babe! It's crazy the way people just speak unendingly into a camera repeatedly, hoping someone will stumble on the video someday. I do not just get the logic of a YouTube channel.

'Hello, welcome to my channel. Today, we are going to talk about relationships.' Like duh, who c…."

"In case you do not know, Adey…" I quickly cut her rant short, "People are making money from this YouTube channel 'craze' as you call it…and hey, it's a happy place sometimes. What I just do not get is why someone should beg me to like or subscribe to their channel. Like, the struggle is real, girl!"

We both laughed hard as we dissed YouTubers who are contributing to mankind by sharing their knowledge with the world- more than we were at the time.

"Wait, let us start our channel! We will call it Lost Wanderers, and we would only just diss people. Gosh, we'd be famous I swear down!"

"Shut up, Adey. You say the craziest things and laugh at yourself. I must go and prep for class. I have just two hours to go. Talk later and be sane till I get back."

Adey always made me feel good. We laugh so intensely at everything that my ex-boyfriend got jealous of our friendship and once told me to stop talking to her because he felt she was not a good influence. It was not true. She is a good person, and besides, I liked Adey too much to stop talking to her because my partner says so. It was simply impossible, so it affected my relationship just a little bit.

38

I got to school thirty minutes before class started and met two other early birds. I said hello but only got a smile as a response, so I thought maybe she was having a quiet time before class. I didn't bother looking at the other girl because I couldn't afford to separate my succulent lips which were nicely resting on each other to give a warm greeting - and all I would get is a forced smile. I soon realized it wasn't a big deal as people would rather share a smile with you than say hello, as opposed to the culture where I was born.

Back home, if you say "Good morning" to someone and they give you just a smile in response, it is considered disrespectful. You must open your mouth to respond. People would ask you if your mouth was too big to respond to a 'common' greeting - and that's how a little thing would lead to unneeded conflict in my country.

I once had a teacher who would respond to every "Good morning" with "Morning" until the principal addressed that response at the assembly. He said it was rude to answer a "Good morning" with just "Morning," (as though it is every time the morning is good). I love Nigeria!

Class over, I went to my favorite joint to get a vanilla milkshake before heading home for a short nap.

***

"Hoooooooonk!" I ran to the other side. thinking it was a big truck honking for me to leave the road. It was a damn tricycle. I could not contain my anger. I stretched out my right hand and spread my five fingers at the driver who most probably did not see my reaction. In Lagos, that is a 'Waka!' sign.

As much as Lagos automatically makes one frustrated due to the traffic, reckless drivers, bad roads, and many other reasons, it always feels good to buy some street food like *boli* and *ekpa* (roasted plantains and groundnuts) while you wait at Allen junction for a bus going to Obalende or wherever you need to go. Some other people may buy gala and an iced Pepsi.

I got into a bus after struggling with people at the bus stop. It is closing hours and I wondered if the working-class population with cars were more than the ones without cars because everywhere was jampacked. When we approach my bus stop, the driver does not stop because of the LASTMA officials stationed at certain points. I protest until I get tired, so I must "exercise patience" as the conductor tells me till, we are clear. It makes me wonder where exactly a bus stop in Lagos is if no parking is allowed on the few ones.

I came out of the bus and back to reality as the door was yanked open by my friend. It was a dream again! I dreamt about Lagos often, and even though I was thankful it was a dream; I truly wanted that experience again.

AT THE TOP

Fill your life with experiences. Not things. Have stories to tell, not stuff to show."

Anonymous

Taxi drivers are the same everywhere. They get unnecessarily happy when your destination is not a stone's throw away. However, the very amazing thing about Dubai taxi drivers which I found very different from Lagos drivers (before the arrival of the Uber) was that most of them were cheerful and ready to mingle even though they worked round the clock, seven days a week.

Whatever happened to the red Lagos metro taxis? It was a breath of fresh air back when they were introduced. They just never got maintained - and that is the problem with Nigeria. Nothing is ever maintained properly. Rather, they die off and something else is brought in, and the cycle continues. I still have hope in the Lagos rail mass transit system, though.

When my friend first told me the train in Dubai was self-driven, I could not imagine it and I did not long to see it either: technology does not thrill me as much. I was patient enough till I was ready to take it, which was about a couple of months after.

My Emirati classmate, Aisha, and I needed to go somewhere, and she thought it would be nice to go by train especially when she heard I had never taken it. As a bougie girl, she topped up her gold card and asked what type of card I would like to purchase, not considering my purse. I decided to go bougie too and asked for the gold card, unknown to me that I would be charged double of what is charged with the silver card.

The train was indeed self-driven. Amazing! But I started to think, what if it stopped? What if something happened? There are no washrooms on it. What if it stopped for about an hour and so many people needed to pee? My colleague laughed at my questions and got people staring at us.

People stare too much on the train. It is as though you have presented them with a special movie, they only had to pay their train fare to watch. It was not until I travelled in the other cabins that I realized that the gold cabin stares were quite minimal. It is like a 4D screen in the other cabins. Tourists are the main actors most times, especially male tourists who step into the women and children's cabin unknowingly. It is usually like a series where you already know what will happen next, but you still want to watch how someone takes the job of the transport staff and rudely informs the tourist they are in the wrong cabin and will be fined if they do not move.

Even though it is a thoughtful thing to warn people, I find it embarrassing because, most times, these tourists do not understand English enough to get the message in time, so the show goes on till they get it. The real show happens when the uniformed staff enters the train to deliberately find and kick out offenders - those who do not tag their cards and those in the wrong cabins.

Also, if you are not smart, you will be told to exit the train for chewing gum. I soon became an offender and never again did it happen to me after that experience:

That fateful day, we had gone on a visit to my friend's tailor. She made me go with her even though I did not want to go. (That is my first advice: never go where you do not want to go.) It happened on our way back. I had no idea I needed to top-up for the bus trip back and there was nowhere around to, so we got on the bus and even sat next to the driver. The effrontery! We were almost at the last stop when the bus was stopped by officials. I continued to pop my gum nonstop, ignorant of what was about to happen.

An officer came on the bus with his machine, and I was the first culprit. I was told to get off the bus and my friend had no choice but to follow. Even though she committed no offense, she was sort of responsible for the situation I found myself in, so she paid the fine and we finished the rest of the journey on foot.

***

Making friends at school was quite difficult as I was the only black girl in class. It took a while before I could understand other girls, especially the Indians and Pakistanis. Aisha did not attend classes regularly because she was busy with family business, so my friend whom I lived with insisted that I explore Dubai a little bit. He purchased some amazing tickets for me, and I decided to use them one at a time. The first place I visited was the top of the Burj Khalifa.

The first question is usually "Where are you from?" followed by "How long have you been in Dubai for?" and the convo goes on and on till either one gets tired. The Pakistani taxi driver told me how much he liked my braided hair and how my skin looked so good. I thought to myself, "I hope this skin still looks good after six months of bathing with the hard water and going out in constant humidity." His accent and inability to speak English properly limited my answers to just one word throughout the trip.

He noticed that I was not saying anything and I saw

how he kept looking at me from the rear-view mirror. "You not angry?" he eventually asked.

Shockingly, I looked at him from the mirror and said "No, but why will you ask that?"

He smiled and then said I did not act like a Nigerian. "You born in America?" he asked with his distorted English as he looked at me.

"No," I replied and smiled at him as I looked away almost immediately wondering why he wanted me to be angry.

He went on to tell me how aggressive Nigerians are and how our accent makes it seem like we are shouting all the time. He asked why I do not have that accent and why I am gentle and concluded that I must have schooled abroad, mixed with some other breed. I wanted to explain to him that my accent was really normal Nigerian accent and that I do not sound American at all because. He would not have believed me, so I just smiled through all his conclusions.

We got to my destination and the meter said I had to pay seven thousand, five hundred naira-equivalent in dirhams for a twenty-minute, no-traffic ride. I inhaled heavily and reached for my purse. I was stuck with the problem of calculating the Naira equivalent of everything I came across for a long time. This indeed is normal and slightly important for anyone who still earns a living in a different currency.

It took me another twenty minutes to walk from the mall entrance to the Burj Khalifa entrance. Unknown to me, there was a long queue that could make one simultaneously hungry and thirsty awaiting me. It reminded me of the car queues at gas stations in Lagos during fuel scarcity. The most frustrating queue ever.

I stood aside trying to figure out what to do - go home or join the queue. I decided to just go to the help desk to at least show my ticket first, and much to my surprise I had a VIP ticket. I was so excited, I smiled with a deep breath of relief as the crowd control was opened for me.

"Me, this black girl, daughter of whom?"

You guessed right. Yes, the daughter of a loving Father who sits in the heavens and makes the earth His footstool.

You should have seen the way everyone in the queue looked at me. I wish I could record that moment and show it to my children whenever I want to teach them how to hold their heads up high. I was already at the top before I even got there.

I got into the fastest elevator in the world and within a

minute, I had that airplane ear feeling like never. I tried every tip I knew to unclog my ears till my cheeks hurt from inhaling a mouth full of air, and I gave up until Mother Nature would release my ears to normal.

I decided to stop at Level 125 and, boy, was it a breath-taking view, literally! As tourists took pictures and had fun, I stood at a corner looking at the view and wondering what the view was like from heaven. Then I went back to Level 124 and bought a few unnecessarily expensive souvenirs. I only wished I had gone later so I could watch the fountain show from the top at night, but the afternoon tea at the café took all that wish away.

I did not want to go back home. I toured the mall a second time on my own and this time, I was not tired of walking even though my feet were hurting a lot.

The next stop was Sephora. That was my first and last time there. It was a splurge that made me wonder what had made me purchase a Dolce and Gabbana matte foundation and perfume kit. What in the name of everything good was I thinking?! I could not understand if it was because of the many YouTube videos I had been watching or my sister's conclusion that I am an impulsive spender or my love for the rich life of getting whatever I wanted even when it is not a life-or-death need.

As though the lady suggesting everything to me knew I was vacillating, she offered me an expensive gift for all I had purchased - just so I would not change my mind. However, as soon as I paid and walked out of their store, I regretted my actions. I wanted it to be another dream, but it was too late.

As I walked out of the mall, I made sure not to look to the left or right, I kept following the signs to take a taxi back home.

On my way home from the Dubai Mall, I could not help calculating and converting all the money I had remaining home and abroad simply because of impulsive shopping but after a while, I took a deep breath and told myself to wear all I bought with optimum grace. That was my reality, even though I still got back home and hid the Sephora bag and other things I had bought for fear of criticism from my friend.

After about a few more weeks, I was getting low on cash and started to look for a job online. I submitted applications every day till depression set in due to the zero response and rejection emails. I started losing weight and people thought I had amazing abs, but it was certainly as a result of hunger and skipping meals because I could not afford them.

Everyone around me started becoming irritating. The feeling of wanting something so badly that nothing else mattered dropped its heavy weight on me. I could barely even do anything at home, so I decided to move out.

Getting a place of my own was a herculean task. Asides from the daunting quest of getting a good deal, the part when landlords say they do not want Africans in their apartment can be quite exasperating. Also, the pictures posted online were not exactly what you saw when you went for a viewing.

In my case, I could only afford a furnished bed space, so I dealt mostly with sketchy middlemen and women who rented apartments directly from landlords and turned them into mini-hostels or "shared apartments", as they call it.

I was able to shortlist a couple of rooms that met my requirements and reached out to the contact numbers provided. However, three out of the five did not want African tenants, and the only reason I could think of was that they just preferred to live with ladies from their own country for better understanding and ease of life. It was not until later that I discovered that landlords and middlemen had always had issues with Africans in the past for many reasons - violence, uncleanliness, and even unpaid rent to name a few. So, I was suffering for the sins of my African brothers and sisters.

After viewing the rooms that welcomed any nationality, I settled for one and moved in before anyone else paid for the space. The decision, however, did not make my situation any better, yet I preferred going through that phase of my life alone than emotionally hurting people who were not responsible for my problems, I thought.

I made several mistakes including not confirming certain things about the apartment - which led me to move out in a couple of months. The apartment was on the twenty-third floor of a building with thirty-three floors, and I was only sharing the room with an Indian girl who ate nothing but leaves of different colors and worried too much about marriage.

Before I moved out, I turned the room into a prayer

altar every day after my roommate left for work. I started to talk to God more and took my quiet time seriously. It is funny how we get closer to God when we need something desperately. I guess this is what getting to the top requires anyways - our need for God's constant help and our ability to always recognize that He can meet every need.

THE JOBS

"There are no shortcuts to the top of the palm tree".

Cameroonian Proverb

My third month in the remarkably contemporary and cosmopolitan city of Dubai was not any better than the second, but a lot of people back home thought I was living my best life. I could not enjoy the city much. I was caught between not wanting to ask my father for more money and being broke because I could not get a job yet. I had a friend who kept inviting me for networking events but after attending a few, I realized that to go out networking, you need to be loaded with some money. Job hunting can be very expensive on its own, especially in a country that is not your own.

I had heard stories of job agents requesting a certain amount from job seekers before securing a job for them. Some never see or hear from the agents anymore. Some job seekers get promised the whole of Dubai but get less than a fraction of what was promised and are stuck with the conditions till they can put together some money to pay up debts. I would rather shop unnecessarily from Sephora than pay an agent to help secure a job.

One particularly cool morning, the seventh day of December to be precise, I was less gloomy, so I said my prayers and had breakfast. Many times, I do not pray when I feel low, and that is a trap no one should ever fall into. It is important to always know that, especially in difficult moments, we should pray on it, over it, and, most importantly, through it.

Usually, I would glance through my emails to see if anyone had sent a reply to me, but I decided to watch a movie and laze around the entire day. Something kept nudging me to check my email, but I did not bother because, for more than a month, I had not gotten any response after applying to a ton of vacancies. I had always been lucky with jobs and applications in Nigeria, so I had thought it would be easy-breezy in a developed country. Alas, it was not.

I still did not feel cast down at noon, something just felt right, and I was in a good place mentally. I thought it must have been the change of weather. That was the best feeling I had had in months. At about noon the next day, I decided to check my email for no reason and, boom! the email the gods of my land had been nudging me to check had been there since nine of the previous morning.

Hi Busola,

Many thanks for your interest in working with us!

Will you be available for a conference call tomorrow at 3:00 pm? If so, on what number should I reach you?

I look forward to hearing from you,

Best,

Antoinette

I was super excited. I could not contain my joy. I ran out of my room and into the corridor that led to the elevators. I pressed on both buttons going up and down. I was not sure how to do it, but I wanted to go somewhere I could scream out loud. I could not wait for the elevator to get to my floor, so I went back to my room and knelt.

My prayers were answered, and I had to move away from a place of comfort to a place where I could think and commune with God. I must have done a praise and dance session for another thirty minutes before I realized that I had not replied to the email.

Hello Antoinette,

Apologies for the late response. Yes, I will be available for a conference call by 3:00 p.m. today.

My mobile number is +971599522222

Regards,

Busola

I got two more interview emails like that after that day, as though the one from Antoinette ushered all of them in. Must have probably been the praise session because I had danced as David danced literally.

It was not until later that I found out that Dubai employers take their time before making decisions. Someone had shared how it took more than ten months from the time he was interviewed for a job to when he started working - and that became clear when I started mine one year after, mainly because I had to negotiate salaries. I lost the offer, finished my six-month course, travelled back home, got the offer again, and resumed work.

***

I could not wait to experience work life in Dubai. In Lagos, whether you own a car or not, the journey to and from work can make you feel like a certified planner. If you live many miles from work, it involves major planning - and can sometimes be a nightmare. If it takes more than an hour, then I guess that you nag and are unhappy most times. While my last job before I moved out of Nigeria was amazing, my everyday situation to and from work was not something I wanted to repeat.

I had a very close friend, Modupeola or Mo as I fondly called her, who was always crying to me about how she was gradually getting tired of the job because she thought it had steadily become a boring routine coupled with no salary raise, no growth in the company, and nothing to look forward to.

This became a norm for us every day. We would get to work an hour before resumption (we always woke up early to meet up with a group of people who worked in the same axis as our office and would pay a subsidized fee to ride together before the rush hour traffic starts). Because it was quite early, we usually expected there would be no traffic or constant stops on the way like regular buses, but on most days, we could not explain why there was bumper-to-bumper traffic. We became a disgruntled working-class family, a set of car-less individuals tired of their jobs but hanging in there because we felt we still had better lives than others who could not put food on their table.

Mo and I would gripe as we applied our makeup in the office; and as other people resumed, they would join in our conversation, also complaining. We soon realized everyone was disgruntled, car-less or not. Sometimes we would forget it was past resumption time and continue our pity-party at breakfast.

The conclusion was that we all hated our jobs, however we needed it to survive. We blamed the government and our bosses for our problems, even though a lot of the blame should have been on us. We loved our comfort zones despite having our energy drained from the morning traffic and constant headaches because of potholes on the expressway.

I had gotten to work once and burst into tears because it felt like my whole life had crashed: I had been robbed on my way to work the previous morning before dawn, by three hoodlums on the next street after mine. I had struggled with them till I was shocked by a slap. One of them snatched the 18K gold necklace and my newly acquired charm bracelet, while a second guy gently removed the Jessica Simpson leopard-skin leather handbag hanging on my right shoulder. A third guy was waiting for them on a motorcycle about five feet away.

They told me not to shout, but I kept saying "Blood of Jesus, Blood of Jesus, Blood of Jesus" till they went away. I wept bitterly like a child, loud enough to awaken the entire neighborhood, but no one came to my rescue for fear of what could happen to them.

I walked back home to cry on my mum's shoulders. She could not contain her anger and ran towards the main road, barefooted, to aid my dad who had gone in pursuit of the robbers. When my dad returned, he drove me to the police station to make a report. I wrote a statement of about two pages explaining what had happened and what I had lost, which included: my white Blackberry phone, which was a luxury at the time, a bottle of 1881 Cerruti perfume for women, my work ID, wallet, debit cards, some mini designer toiletries, and a lot of garbage that was in my handbag for no reason.

The police station was an eyesore. Despite being there very early, a woman was already detained for beating up her boyfriend who had cheated on her with his supposed wife. As I waited for my dad, her case made me forget totally about my problems. I cannot remember what bothered me more - the silly case, the police officers on duty who spoke with so much insolence, or the noise coming from the cells in the backyard. We left the police station with some hope but, sadly, we never heard from them till date.

When I got to work the day after the incident, I burst into tears. Not because I had been robbed, but because it would not have happened if I did not need to leave home for work before dawn. I hated the job more and did not go to work for a week. However, I soon got tired of staying at home so I braced up, and even though I was still terrified I continued to leave home before daybreak this time in the company of a tricycle driver who would drive me to the major road every morning.

Moving to closer proximity to my work was not an option because I was a proper Nigerian girl born to a protective Yoruba father who did not want me living outside his home till marriage. Being a young Nigerian woman can be quite daunting sometimes, with uncanny cultural values that continue to limit the girl child.

At the office, the only time we put more effort into our work was one time when there was a vacant managerial position in my department. All eight of us suddenly became better at our jobs, until we got an email informing us that a European expatriate would be filling the position in a couple of weeks.

We became disgruntled again.

"What rubbish! I heard the guy is twenty-three years old, Busola," Mo had sent me an email one afternoon with lots of crying emojis. She titled the mail "I HATE THIS JOB." I could feel her hurt from the e-mail.

"Take it easy Mo, the light will shine on us soon," I replied to her, giving them hope like I always did.

"Who knows, he might have an older friend he can introduce you to, and then you will finally have all

63

you've wanted."

"SILLY!!! Let's go see a movie tonight."

Going to see a movie meant that we would have to sort out extra transportation to the movies and back home. We booked a cab and as we started our ride, Mo got an SMS and the whining started again. Mo hated it when things did not add up. She sighed heavily and I paused from scrolling through my Instagram timeline to give her my attention.

"What now?"

"I wonder why it's okay for him to have lots of female friends but it's a problem when I post pictures with my male friends on Instagram," she said with disgust. She had been dating Dekunle for two years and some months, and they seemed to be a happy couple to me until that evening.

"Dekunle said that to you?"

"What sort of generation are we in, jeez?"

"Whao!" I kept chipping in my disappointment from time to time as she revealed their issues.

"I'm sorry about all of these, Mo, but if you've stayed with him for two years, then it means you are fine with it all; so, stop complaining or, better still, leave if it worries you this much." I was always unnecessarily blunt with my responses to issues.

"This is why you do not have a boyfriend, B. There are some things you cannot change about men, and it has to do with their ego…" She got me so angry with this statement that I did not know when I used the 'F' word and interrupted her abruptly.

We could not change our minds about the movie as we had already made payments, so we watched like two broken lovers. The ride home was the quietest ever and the traffic even made it worse. Our friendship ended that day.

The enemies one makes at work can also be very interesting when you begin to analyze how the enmity started. I once had a co-worker ask me why it was when I started working in the company that the IT guy knew he was ready for a relationship.

"…as though no pretty girls were working here before you came," she said once, giving me a look that could tear my dress off my body. These were unnecessary problems that came with my job at the time: too many people disliked me for no major reason, rumors abounded about me kissing the said IT guy in the pantry, and there was constant misuse of power by team leads.

I could not wait to compare working in Dubai to Lagos even though the thoughts of cultural diversity gave me anxiety.

After a few back and forth with the lady who sent the mail, I did not take the job offer in Dubai. Neither did I get other jobs. So, I was back to square one and left with no choice but to call Daddy. For two more months I was okay but then decided to stop searching for jobs altogether and just focus on going back home. I missed my family, even though they all wanted me to remain in Dubai. I was always filled with nostalgia for Lagos.

BEAUTIFUL, COLORFUL

"In the midst of difficulty lies opportunity".

Albert Einstein

The first time I left my family, it was not a cheerful day, there was a mixture of despair and delight all in one, like day and night struggling to stay together. I wished I could change my plans and stay with my family, but life had to continue no matter what.

We got to the airport three hours before check-in and for the first time, I was the one going through the check-in queue, weighing my luggage, and completing the immigration form. I was usually the one who escorted everyone travelling abroad and kept them company till it was time to board. I knew almost all the restaurants at the Murtala Mohammed International Airport, Lagos. For some reason, I was always denied a visa even before I turned the legal adult age so all I could do was get to the airport and return home. I never crossed over. Very frustrating.

I always wondered why the airport was never scanty and watched people who either rolled their lush luggage or pulled on their worn-out, Ghana-must-go bags.

"I hope you did not collect anything from anybody and where are the keys to the padlocks I gave you to lock your bags?"

My dad asked more questions than the immigration officials asked me.

"Jeez, I got this!".

"O da ma 'jeez' nbe. This is your first time travelling, don't deceive yourself and shine your eyes." We all laughed.

That day felt completely surreal. My dad had tears welled up in his eyes just like the day we buried Mum. I had mixed feelings: excited about my first trip outside my motherland, sad that I was supposed to go on the trip with my mum, overwhelmed by thoughts of missing my siblings and entire family, and upset because my partner wanted to see me at all costs, but it had not just been possible.

Soon, I hugged my dad and sister after another round of soft prayers before I moved on with my carry-on luggage to the immigration checkpoint. The prayers never end, my oldest sister had led the prayer the evening before we left for the airport, and then my dad had added a few prayer points. I could hear his voice shaking and, at that point, I felt I had made the wrong decision to leave my family at a most difficult time. We shrugged off the emotional moment soon after the prayers as my dad reminded us all that it was for a great cause.

There was a fourth round of prayers before I finally went to board my flight.

The guy next to me looked like he left home after a cool shower and a meal. His wife must have sorted him out for his seven-hour flight in all ways, I thought as I stared for a couple of seconds at the way his wedding ring clasped his ring finger. He helped me with my seat belt and headphones. I was not going to pretend I knew how to handle things and fumble my way through. Sure, I could act like I had it all together, but I did not bother.

Then we started talking. His fruity voice kept sending all the wrong signals into my heart, but I was smart enough to hear him with my brain and not my heart. We talked about his first flight and how it was very easy. He had been flying regularly since he became an entrepreneur, and his business took him around the world every month. He kept talking, but I was constantly distracted by his wedding ring as though there was a charm on it that kept reminding me to keep it simple because he was married.

He, however, didn't seem like the type of man to be interested in taking advantage of a young naïve girl who seemed to just be starting in life. He dozed off at some point and did not even wake up to eat, probably because he still had another flight to catch at DXB. I managed to do every other thing by myself till we got to our destination.

I had been informed to connect to the free Wi-Fi at the airport when I arrived so I could communicate my safe arrival to my sleepless family. I thought about how nice it would be to have free Wi-Fi in Nigerian airports, but then I remembered how we had to pay for a trolley and shrugged off the thought.

The decision to leave home was not an easy one especially with the way things were. I had to leave a lot of things behind to take a step of faith into the unknown at a very low moment. Staying positive was more important than how I was feeling because perhaps it was destiny. My Yoruba people will say, "Akosile ni" meaning "It has already been prewritten".

I had attended too many motivating seminars that

inspired me to want more from life and stay positive on the journey. I have all the schools I attended to thank for that. The day a motivational speaker came to my secondary school just before we graduated, he taught us a song that will remain fresh in my heart forever:

Beautiful Colorful I must get there

Beautiful Colorful I will get there

My future is bright I must get there.

Even though I do not remember most of the things he said that day, those lyrics remained engraved on my heart mostly because I believed in them a lot and they always gave me the courage and confidence to try harder and do more, especially during low moments.

-

After my short course was over in Dubai, I was happy that I could finally go back home to my family, even though my visa was still valid for another six months. Apart from the fact that I was extremely homesick, I was having a hard time deciding whether to go back to Nigeria where I could make better use of all I had learned from my six months study or stay back without any good source of income, continuing to struggle with endless "*we are sorry we will be moving forward with another candidate*" emails.

Then I thought about the struggle in Lagos, the mosquitoes, and the yellow buses I would be going back to, and I broke down in tears. Days went by before I could even completely decide. I started to feel bad for not taking previous job offers and blamed myself for having a high standard with the little-or-no experience resume I had. I wondered why I had negotiated salaries unnecessarily and wrote back to Antoinette several times, asking her if she still needed me and telling her how I was willing to take the salary she was offering. I got no feedback from her. I went for more interviews and more interviews, and it was crickets afterward.

I hated sitting at home or roaming the streets of Dubai with no source of income especially because nothing came free in Dubai, not even your attempt to have fun at home with friends. There was also the guilt you feel when you go to parties or tried to have fun with friends who have jobs. It was just a complete torture of the mind.

The only thing that kept me busy was church. I would

be the first to get to all the church programs and the last to leave. Even though I had reservations as to why there had to be church activities on four days of the week, I could not complain much because I had nowhere else to go.

When I got tired and bored out of my skull, I decided to apply for jobs back home and, within a few days of several applications, I got a job offer.

I was super excited about this new job. It was like a dream come true. I had practiced how to relate with my new colleagues and ways to make them like me. I made sure I always had sweet or chewing gum on me that would make them always come to me. Unfortunately, I made more enemies than friends simply because they were told I was hired from Dubai to be a supervisor. I immediately understood their plight as this had once been my case also.

Two months into the job, I started to regret my decision to return home. My boss was very temperamental and I was now used to the easy life so work was tough. I was not sure if she also started to resent me because I was taking life easily or whether she was just pathetic at managing people.

On a Monday morning, which was supposed to be my day off, she had fixed an appointment. I waited in her office for about four hours, and she never called to change the time, nor did she leave me a message whatsoever. Considering I was not getting an extra day to replace it, she just could not be bothered.

After waiting needlessly for hours, I said a prayer to God. "Dear Lord, when I finally get to this position, help me to respect and care for my subordinates and co-workers."

I then picked up my phone and sent her a message. Her reply came in thirty minutes later with a message for me to meet her somewhere that would take me an hour to get to. I do not know where the courage came from, but I replied to her saying that I would see her the next day instead. I later found out she had been busy with a photoshoot, but I could care less - her life seemed haphazard, and I just could not deal.

She had to be the rudest human wrapped in a beautiful body that I had ever had the 'honor' of meeting in my entire life. Many times, her beauty quickly faded when she started cussing the living daylights out of her workers, including those old enough to birth her father.

She used the 'F' word more than I had ever heard in my years on earth and I started to see it as a norm. This was until the day she cussed me out.

Everyone condoned and feared her, but I did not. Some even said she was born with a silver spoon by a strict father and that was why she behaved that way. Oh well, I was born with a diamond spoon from a loving father. How did I not turn out spoilt? Duh.

I always felt I should speak with her like a sister because the only reason I could not love the job was her pathetic attitude. However, she never gave room for small talk. After another month at the job, she insulted me, called me "lazy" and other names that made my head spin fast in a space that had nothing less than five hundred people present. Oh! The nerve she had, to call me names when all I was trying to do was get the job done!

That was when I lost it. I lashed out at her, and I never believed my benign voice could rise and travel so fast. The earth stood still, everyone stopped, and I became the cynosure of all eyes. My colleagues could not believe that it would be the little not-so-outspoken Busola that would face the uncouth boss.

I knew I had lost my dream job when her driver took me to a corner and told me that day to forget the job and my salary for the month, go home and move on with my life.

Even though I continued working with her for about one more month, it was glaring that she did not know the best way to let go of me but soon, she quietly removed me from the group chat and that was it, my dream job ended. It was painful, more so because I loved that job and risked my safety many times to get the job done.

But sometimes, the hardest roads lead to the best places: I was grateful for the hard time she gave me. It left me with no option but to get outside the box and look ahead as Dubai called to me again with doors wide open.

My capacity was built, and I learned that nobody is perfect. We are all on a journey to a beautiful and colorful place.

SHE SLEPT, WE AWOKE

It is better to go to the house of mourning than to go to the house of feasting, for that [day of death] is the end of every man, And the living will take it to heart and solemnly ponder its meaning.

Ecclesiastes 7:2 AMP

It was time to go back to Dubai and this time, my dad was the happiest. "Go to your mum's grave and tell her you're leaving," he said, looking away. He hates to look into our eyes when he wants to talk about mummy. What I would never understand is why I must always go speak to the pretty-looking grave that is not my mum.

I just felt all I needed was her spirit which is always with me anyway, so why tell someone that you feel around you every time that you are going somewhere? Rolling my eyes as always, I obeyed him, not only because I wanted to obey, but because I had a little belief that she sits there whenever we are there.

Few weeks after she was buried, my sister's newborn who had never met his grandma always found comfort at her grave for some reason. He would cry like a precious toy had been taken away from him each time we dragged him away from the graveside. We all concluded there must be something extraordinary about that, even though I still thought it was because the grave looked like a very cool playground for him. My dad had

79

been particular about the design. "It's the least I can do for a peaceful rest," he would always say.

Mummy's health continued to fail. She had been sick for a year and some months, losing more weight with every passing day. She was a very strong woman, an early riser, and a devoted nurturer even in sickness. She had never been sick for more than a day or two until then, and so we took her sickness for granted the first few months. Her preference for trado-medicine made her use so many disgusting and smelly herbs that initially seemed promising.

When we finally agreed that her health needed urgent attention, everyone started to talk in hushed tones.

"What exactly is the problem?" I would often ask.

"Ko le ye ẹ Busola. Iwọ sha ma wo n ti ẹ." She felt I was too young to understand why she was so sick and not getting better. She was in so much pain but appeared super strong. She went to the hospital only a couple of times and each time I asked what the doctor said, she would just shrug it off and act as though it was not that serious. She practically protected her children from her non-contagious sickness. She also stopped going to the hospital because she was told she would die if she stayed there.

I noticed that her regular meals had reduced to once a day. She only preferred to stay in her room, stopped watching her favorite shows and had started calling me over the phone instead of just yelling my name like she always did - I knew I had to press her to talk to me.

She finally told me what the problem was, and my brain suddenly froze. I was somewhere in between disappointed and upset. "Ovarian cyst! Dear Lord."

I started to read far and wide. I joined a plant-based health company to buy healthier products that resembled herbs since she liked them so much. I started to love her more as she slowly became my child. Taking care of her made me realize the length I would go to for someone I love. I did not even know I loved her that much because we quarreled every other day over the most mundane things. One time we quarreled over her Burberry scarf. I told her she was not my mother just because she would not let me use the scarf, and she told me to go find my mother somewhere else and collect her scarf instead. Ugh, she had a way of getting under my skin.

When she became sick, I was ready to be her strength, and that I was till the very last day. On the ninth day of the ninth month, it was my turn to go say hello to her at the hospital. My dad had told me what to bring for her and I was ready, I was hopeful, and I believed she would get well. I got to the specialist hospital in Victoria Island, and I loved the serenity. I immediately felt that my mum would get better; but when I saw my dad, he was unnecessarily quiet as I greeted him. His gray hair was not looking neat, and he had lost a few pounds. He had been spending the night with her for days.

"Ma sunkun o, Busola. Mummy has passed on to glory," he finally found his voice. He said it once, but I processed it many times before I understood what he meant.

I sat down for a moment and could not find tears. I was there watching as he kept calling my mum's family members to tell them the news. I thought that when you hear of a loved one's death, the next thing would be to wail like in the movies, but my dad was acting so normal, I was confused. I felt like I was in a different world - people were moving but I did not see them. The only person I saw and heard was my dad.

Everything seemed abnormal for a while. I could not express any form of emotion, so I just sat still. Then a nurse came in and my dad introduced her to me. She asked if I would like to see my mum, and for the first time since I arrived at the hospital, I remembered why I was there in the first place.

"Yes, of course," I mumbled, and I stood up to follow her.

We went up the stairs and I looked down at my dad countless times. When we got to her room, the nurse opened the door and pressed some sanitizer on my hands. The fan was blowing very cool air, the room was neat, and I saw equipment that I had only seen in movies. They reminded me of the dream my mum had told me she had had a few days earlier: She had been taken to a room full of surgical equipment like the ones I was just seeing by her side. She said she had recognized the doctor and the surgery had been successful. This dream had given us some hope before she was taken to the hospital.

However, here I was in this room, my mum covered in white garments. The nurse asked if I was ready to see her face. I nodded, still not able to show any form of emotion.

Suddenly, I felt slightly joyful when I saw her face - and then I felt pain when I saw the cotton balls in her nose and ears. She looked a lot more relaxed than the last time I saw her. The hair on her head was in the cornrow style I had last made for her. I touched her hand and opened my mouth, but no words could come out except for a gasp that came out like a heavy sigh. I looked at her for so long, yet I still could not shed a tear. Then the nurse asked if I was ready to leave. I looked at the nurse, then back at my mum, gave that deep sigh again, and nodded my head.

As soon as she covered my mum's face and we walked out of the room, the tears rolled down uncontrollably for hours nonstop. I walked out of the hospital into the parking lot so I could cry louder, and then I sent a message to my sister who was asleep far away in Boston Massachusetts to help me. I thought I had lost my very own life. I thought that was the end of life.

When I did not get a response from her immediately, I called my partner and wept bitterly on the phone.

"She left me without even saying goodbye. Why?"

He became helpless and I never really heard all he said

to comfort me till the call dropped.

I then wiped my tears when I saw my dad and his friends approaching – I didn't want him to see me broken because it might break him more. The ambulance had arrived to take her to the morgue and I saw them put her body in the van and the siren was turned on immediately. We all left in a convoy to the morgue.

There, at the mortuary, I saw a lot of things that made me sick to my stomach. There was a newly dead body lying on the back seat of a car with rolled-down windows. A lady sat a few steps away from the car crying – I did not even know how to feel with this sight because one minute I was mortified and the next minute, I was full of pity. It must have either been her husband, brother, or partner, but I sincerely felt her pain. My dad greeted her, but we had to sort ours out.

I thought the workers at the morgue were hard-hearted, but since this was their job, they must have been trained to face everything they saw. We paid for a long list of things, and it was at that point - when they put her on the roller and removed the white garment - that I broke down. I was shattered to the very last piece of me, and this broke my dad too. We both cried like babies. That was when I knew I was never seeing my mother again. I took all her hospital bags and held them close like it was her and did not speak to my dad or anyone till we got home.

Getting home was another round of confusion for me. Everyone was now at home, waiting for us. I got in angrily and did not say a word to anybody until we were all gathered to pray.

That same day, my oldest brother-in-law convinced my dad that we must inform my brother who lived in London. Then my second sister got angry and started shouting because she felt there would be no one to comfort my brother where he was. I kept looking at all of them and all I could think of was how I would not see my best friend again. The chaos that comes with not knowing what to do filled our home. They finally agreed to call him, and my brother lost it over the phone. He wept like a little child till the call ended.

That night was the scariest and longest night ever. I could not sleep. The only person I liked to sleep next to when I could not sleep was gone.

Days went by and our family drew closer like never before. The devotional we used every morning for about a week was coincidentally teaching loss. We were comforted in all ways till the day we laid her body to rest in that beautiful grave daddy built her.

The only thing that comforted me was my threat to her on her last Mother's Day. I had paid some money for us to hang out with some other mothers and their children at a Mother's Day event. Even though she was sick and had lost so much weight, she summoned the courage to go with me. I saw the happiness on her face, and it brought unexplainable joy to my heart. I would give anything to do that with her repeatedly.

Her death was our awakening: that was when I started to grow up; we learned to take our health seriously from then on; we all became more spiritually focused, and we lived every day loving and supporting each other more.

Did it have to take the loss of a loved one before we woke up from our slumber? Maybe. I do not know. That might have been one of God's unquestionable ways.

And as though to test our awakening and faith, I found

a lump in my breast a few months after she passed. It felt like affliction had risen a second time. I could not tell anyone about my sleepless nights. I just wanted to pray it out, and, oh dear! I prayed and fasted – yet it remained.

I read all I could about breast lumps and all I saw was cancer even though there were also benign explanations.

My faith was tested, and I almost gave up till I found the courage to tell my sister. It did not even help that I was many miles away from my family and all alone. I thought I was going to die. I even wanted to help myself die quickly and had many suicidal thoughts because I was not only dealing with this lump, but I was also going through an emotional crisis in my relationship. Nothing seemed to be working anymore and all I could think of was going to be with my mum. However, I never got around to killing myself because I was more afraid to die than I was afraid of my predicament.

After my dad found out about my condition, he was terrified and asked that I returned home. We found a specialist hospital where I was constantly going for mammograms and checks. Hospitals brought back sad memories for all of us, but we were strong for each other. I was told I had the option of checking the lump to see if it was cancerous or not - which meant that if it was not cancerous, I might just live with a lump for a while till it decided to disappear on its own, or I could remove it instantly whether it was cancerous or not.

My thoughts started running wild: What other things could be going on in my body that I was not aware of? Are my ovaries, okay? What about my womb and cervix? Oh no, my liver! Do I have any trace of diabetes?

I was too nervous to think positive thoughts; notwithstanding, I just wanted the lump out of my breast even though it caused me no pain or discomfort. So, we opted for a lumpectomy.

Life started dishing lots of issues my way in this difficult time. I lost a lot of friends. I lost my relationship and I lost myself especially when the surgical site got infected and stopped healing. I had to go through a new set of stitches - this time without anesthesia.

I went through what seemed like hell. I was alone in the hospital for the second stitching, and I wept bitterly. I had no one to support me because it was the same day my sister was getting introduced at home.

At one point, I closed my eyes and saw my mum. She was right there with me, giving me all the comfort, I needed to push through the pain. I felt a sudden peace around me and thought I had died and gone to heaven - until the doctor told me he was done.

I knew I had lost my mum physically, but I was convinced since that day that she became an angel that would never leave, and who would always help me push through life. She became my solace, the only one I could talk to; and even though she would not talk back, it was okay. I wrote to her every time I wanted to talk to someone, and most of the time I would feel her presence, though at other times I would not. One of the letters I wrote made me laugh and cry a lot at the same time.

Dear Victoria,

I cannot remember my toddler years but seeing the way you cared for your grandbabies, I know you gave me ALL the love that you could give.

How you made amala and ewedu taste like a miracle is still a wonder to me.

The watery Yoruba stew though! Hahaha!

I was not joking every time I sang that I would buy you a car and build you two houses in Ghana. I will still do it for you mama.

Remember when you told me I would marry a fine rich man? Can you tell me if he loves God and would do everything right by God only? I think I have met this man though. He fits all you told me, but he is too sweet? How can a human being be so sweet despite all I do to deliberately hurt his feelings (I know, but I am sorry).

I miss braiding your hair and the shocking slaps you give me when I chew gum while at it - how you sleep off so peacefully.

I miss how you press on your phone and how you end the call immediately you are done talking even if the other person is not done, only to get a call back - you are too funny.

I miss how you say "stupid" (Doyin and I still say "stupid" that way) and how you call me "tortio" when I start to act sluggish, and how you call me "my babe."

I miss how you tell me to reduce my sugar intake but still go on and buy me cake and chin chin on Tuesdays.

Mum, I never got to tell you about my deepest heartaches. I never got to share my real, depressing problems with you because I knew you might not be able to take it.

You were so proud of me and I know you still are, but after you passed, I got rebellious. Mummy, I did things you would not have been proud of, and I am sorry. I always imagine you begging God on my behalf in heaven - so surreal.

I want you to know, Mummy, that I love you and I will always remember every piece of advice you gave me. I am still trying to figure out why you said I should not marry a white man though, but I will not. I love you Mummy, and I am glad I told you that when you were with me.

MY AFRICA

"If you followed the media, you'd think that everybody in Africa was starving to death, and that's not the case; so, it's important to engage with the other Africa".

Chimamanda Ngozi Adichie

I was now back in Dubai and could sleep better on my own. I had moved into my fourth shared apartment and, this time, I shared a room with a Russian girl who did not seem nice for the first few weeks I lived there, until the day we finally had the chance to have a heart-to-heart talk.

I was on the phone with Adey and we talked about our trip to Zanzibar. We were planning this trip that we still had not embarked on for more than a year with so much excitement.

After my call, my roommate was curious to know why I was happier than normal as she kept stealing glances at me before summoning the courage to ask. I then told her how I had been wanting to visit Zanzibar for the past two years.

She asked where Zanzibar was, and after I explained to her, she was concerned as to why an African girl would be thrilled to go visiting Africa. The notion that Africa is one country needs to be abolished from our planet – I will not even expect an alien from Venus to think such a thing in this century. She gave me a turned-up nose that portrayed her disapproval like she did when I first cooked my special efo-riro in her presence. She started to tell me how I was the first African she ever lived with. She then recounted her first experience of setting eyes on black people:

She had moved to America two years earlier for greener pastures and as she got to the airport, she decided to freshen up in the restroom. Unknown to her that she had entered the men's restroom, she started brushing her teeth and as she looked up into the mirror after the first rinse of her mouth, she saw two black guys walking in on her. She became afraid and ran out at the speed of light, leaving behind her luggage and everything she had on her. She said the guys watched her as if she was mentally disturbed and shook their heads with so much disgust on their faces. She thought they had come in to rape her, in broad daylight, at the airport. Ugh.

My adrenaline slowly delved into a faint fury after her reaction to my Zanzibar update and her forlorn story. I was concerned about the narrative of Africa that she had, and though I knew that I could not do much to change it at that moment, I still tried. I felt the need to make her understand that Africa is more than what she thought she knew. We sat, and the discussion went on and on. That was the longest we had spoken since I moved into the apartment.

She explained the Africa she saw in movies and the one from the news, and this got me feeling like I needed to educate her. She told me about the little black children loitering streets and how that had become her mental picture of Africa. It is always the little black children and the garbage pictures!

I explained what the media had chosen to feed the public all the time to make money and what I knew the reality to be – in a way that she would understand that there was a remarkable difference. I also told her that, without a doubt, we had our problems, and I used our energy supply crisis in Nigeria as an instance.

Her reaction when I dramatized the sudden power outage was hilarious. I stood up and turned off the power and air conditioner switch so that it was now dark and hot. I said, "Imagine this happened and it's not restored until three or more days later - and when it's restored, it goes out again for a few more hours."

She gasped as though I was taking her breath away.

"Like a horror movie?"

"Exactly. Like a horror movie, but people just move on with their alternative power supply like a generator or inverter, and those that cannot afford an alternative, will have to wait till power is restored."

Her eyes nearly popped out and I realized that I may have worsened her notion of Africa. So, to salvage all my dramatic explanations, I went further to educate her on how I love my country despite its inadequacies. I did a lot of comparisons: how the rent we paid monthly for our room could get us a 2-BHK for one full year in Nigeria.

She marveled, and I felt a bit better as I watched her emotions transform from time to time. I made her see Africa in a new light - but I also felt like I had lied to myself half of the time.

I know that Nigeria suffers from abject poverty. In most parts of the city of Lagos, a middle-class family can have a poverty-stricken family as their next-door neighbor. The unroofed and unpainted home of the poor family who eats the same meal almost every day sits right beside a double-coated semi-detached home of the middle-class family who own at least two cars.

Nigeria is however rich in agriculture and natural resources. Although some hybrid animals have been reported to swallow hard currency from time to time, we are blessed with organic produce.

I was intentional about giving her a balanced story so she at least knows that there is some good in Nigeria or Africa as a continent.

I also addressed her story because she worried about her reaction being racist and I told her about how racism is a sad reality that we have to deal with outside our country I added that until I moved - even though I have experienced the challenges that follow tribalism and ethnicity in Nigeria, I had never known how intense racism was. More than being racist, I told her she was densely ignorant of the nuances and challenges of having a different skin colour.

My roommate and I got closer and talked about everything. We talked about our food, culture, and everything in between. She also wanted to know everything about my relationship, how I coped with Christianity in Dubai.

She was very curious about the level of my moral standing and how I was able to get myself to that stage. She got comfortable enough to tell me how she had been married once and gotten divorced because she could not cope with the way their love "vanished" after a few months.

"It was too stressful: he stopped helping out and I couldn't do everything for two people on my own," she said. She then advised me to make sure that my partner was someone I could be with through thick and thin before agreeing to marry him.

Marriage seems to be getting tougher with every passing generation. I thought. but I have never doubted that it can equally work out with God's help but no one should pretend they are enjoying a life-threatening union for any reason whatsoever.

My roommate then went on to tell me how much she loved Davido and Nigerian music - as though Davido himself was a special genre of music. If she disagreed with anything else, Nigerian music always saved the image of Africa as they topped all her playlists.

GRACE

"Never explain - your friends do not need it and your enemies will not believe you anyway".

Elbert Hubbard

The sky looked very cloudy - not like it would rain, but a different type of cloudy. I sat at my desk staring deeply into the sky as though I was getting some sort of strength from it. I became absent-minded in a few minutes after I lost internet connection and when it suddenly came back, there was a loud sound from my computer that made me shake for a second. I was startled. I had left YouTube playing my favorite songs from a playlist it had created for me and I smiled as I continued to sing along.

Each day, the weather was different. I had a very amazing view at work that gave me the privilege of looking into the sky, and I loved that I could see one of the tallest buildings in the world every day.

The hygiene staff at my office came up the elevator and stood by my desk because she also noticed that there was something different about the weather. "It looks like there'll be a sandstorm." She said this with a smile and knocked on the desk.

I smiled back without saying a word. Not because I did not want to reply to her but because I just did not have any reply for her. I had always wondered why she would knock on wood whenever she said anything. I thought she was very strange until someone else knocked on wood after complimenting my beautiful and smooth skin once.

I got curious enough to Google it and found there was a term for the act - "Touchwood." It is believed that spirits live in woods and so you touch or knock-on-wood to prevent or distract the spirits from hearing your hopes for the future, else they would jinx the good things you have said, and it will not come true - or if you have said anything negative, the touch on wood prevents the spirits from acting on it.

My mind began to wander off again. "Sandstorm"?! Why on earth would she think that a somewhat cloudy sky is a sign of a sandstorm? Where was the link?

After about an hour, I got a message on my phone:

Hey beautiful, I have 2 tickets to the Hillsong concert tonight at 7 p.m. I will pick you up at 6:45 p.m. Be ready.

Grace's messages always made me smile, and even though I was excited by the content of the message, I shook my head and rolled my eyes because she did not even care to ask if I had made some other plans for the night.

I loved Grace just like I loved Adey. Grace was thirty-three, very intelligent, and single. I particularly fancied her mantra, "I am enough for myself". The company she worked for in Nigeria had moved two of their staff to Dubai as a form of promotion - she and another colleague. However, the other person was not allowed to move because his medical result came with a trace of tuberculosis. I admired Grace's love for God and I think it was that love in her that made me love her so much.

She picked me up after work and we drove to get dinner at Mc Donald's before setting out to the concert. The Dubai Duty-Free tennis court was already packed to the brim with mostly Filipinos chit-chatting before the event even started. The only available space left was the overflow section where we had to stand all through the event. The Dubai Police roamed the venue to ensure crowd control and safety and the concert was phenomenal with all hands raised and all hearts fixed on God.

After the phenomenal event with what looked like the

whole of Dubai in attendance for the two days, I got back home. As I sat on my bed, I felt grains of sand. There had really been a sandstorm and it rained sand in my flat. I was perplexed as I remembered my colleague who had mentioned it earlier – *so much for touching wood,* I thought. My flat mates had however been nice enough to call the cleaners to clean the entire flat before I returned but I still had to take care of the little bit left on my sheets.

I finally finished cleaning and laid down to rest. Before I shut my eyes to sleep, I reflected on the concert and how thousands of Christians had gathered to worship God in a Muslim space. It felt surreal. I could not be prouder of the Dubai government and how receptive they are of Christianity in all its form and glory - apparently after millions of permissions and protocols.

***

There are several churches in Dubai for people of the Christian faith. Apart from some other Pentecostals that rent hotel ballrooms to gather saints together, I had seen Arab Evangelical Church Dubai (AECB), St. Francis of Assisi Catholic Church, and United Christian Church of Dubai; but I never worshipped at any of these mainly because I had the opportunity of worshipping with Nigerians in a ballroom every Friday before it became a normal Sunday situation.

I loved my church a lot. I had even joined the media team and became Amanpour Junior in my head as I served as the news anchor. The cameraman who was my very good friend would hype me and all the news anchors so much that it made us want to do better the next time. It was an honor to be of service to God and man in such a beautiful way.

However, people started to leave the church - this was asides those that moved out of the city. I could not understand when a friend I had just made in church stopped attending. He said it was because he was constantly having to deal with rumors, negativity, and criticisms. I was gutted, I thought he was over reacting because people talk everywhere even at work, so should we stop going to work because colleagues have a false narrative of us? I wanted him to tell me more about it because I just could not wrap my head around it at the time - until I experienced my fair share of church hurt.

It was a simple reason: Human beings will always be human. I finally understood why people stopped attending and why they would rather worship online. Negativity feels different when it is coming from the church.

Human beings always have more expectations of other people than they have of themselves, and so they hurt people with idle talks - sometimes unintentionally, and many times intentionally - because that habit of casting stones when they have seen or heard something about another person helps them get by their problems. They begin to weigh each other's sins and create unnecessary double standards.

The church started to hurt me more than the issues I was facing daily. A rumor had gone around that the girl who read the news in the church was living with the guy from her team, who did illegal business for work - and we all know what that means in a church: it also silently meant that they must be intimate. So, I started to feel intimidated like the woman by the well. I felt that way because the rumor had some elements of truth but that was my business, right?

I was living with a young man that I was not married to, which I never really saw as a big deal except because it was against the law and I could be assaulted for it at the time (thankfully that law has now been amended and cohabitation is legal). I was not happy that my truth was out there, and worse still in the church. We had just started dating privately and he had travelled outside Dubai for some business while I stayed over at his to save myself rent but people got so judgmental that they said things that satisfied their curiosity.

He was a good guy that did not deserve any shame regardless of what his past or present at the time may have been. This caused a strain between us, and so we could not have the best of relationships that we both truly deserved, whether we were meant to be or not.

I moved out of his house and broke up with him, thinking the rumors would die down - but they had only just started with me. I remember receiving a call from a "sister" in church one day, pretending to check on my welfare. She asked after my friend who had moved out of Dubai to be with her boyfriend in America and talked about how that was not a good decision then went on to tell me that she heard I was also living with a guy. I wanted to end the call but I respected her. She told me that everyone was talking about me dating a guy no one approved of. That call shattered me more than I was already broken as she had given me a sermon about love and the right way to do things – so much from someone whose got married some years later and her marriage ended shortly.

I realized that I was also culpable of misjudging people based on half stories and hearsays. Someone said, "Once you stop judging others, you'll stop judging yourself as well. That's when the healing and goodness you've felt undeserving of will start to flow."

From then on, I made a promise to slow down on reacting to one sided stories or gist as we call it, because I now understood how it felt.

A few months went by, and I was back in the relationship people were unhappy about, simply because I stopped judging myself based on people's judgment. I knew it was my life, and only I understood my situation as well as the importance of my happiness, but still, they kept getting in my head every single time. I heard all sorts of terrible things about this guy that my heart had chosen to love without my permission, and this messed up my mind a lot. I was now caught between my heart and my mind. I became unnecessarily overprotective of myself for months, and even though we had our separate issues, the ones that stemmed from the church were more overwhelming.

I had broken up with him three times in a year based on trivial issues. I became a monster that caused trouble and loved to fight every single time there was an opportunity, I never respected him for another minute, and I had even used my stand for feminism against him – terrific.

Something about me had changed. The church no longer felt comfortable, so, I decided to leave. I was away for months, tried other churches, but carried my hurt with me so there was no way for me to heal. Eventually, I healed slowly on my own with the help of God from an online sermon that was titled "When Church Hurts". I watched the sermon over and over again till I felt better in my spirit and after I had healed to an extent, I knew it in my spirit that I needed to go back to my church. There is nothing like fellowshipping with saints and there was no reason to attend a new church because, according to that sermon, they will hurt you at that new church as well. Also, because I could not further allow people's expectations to move me out of God's instruction, I went back to church. Even though the stigma was still there, I lived through it and found my peace again.

Someone said, "They had your best interest at heart but communicated it in the wrong way." Quite honestly, no one can ever want the best for someone else more than God does or more than they do for themselves, so people need to learn to slow down - even though we all need these crazy things to happen sometimes so we can be stronger and wiser.

I believe Christians should learn to pray for people rather than set a table of slander for those they feel are not 'Christian' enough - and if they cannot find a way to pray for their loved ones or enemies, it is advisable to keep quiet in order not to lose their own salvation. Silence, they say, is golden but "the grace of God is everything and more."

MY FAIR SHARE OF YORUBA MEN

"The most important thing for a young man is to establish a creditable reputation, character".

John Rockefeller

God must have known what I needed because Adey was now planning to move to Dubai.

After what felt like eternity, my best friend of five years whom I have lost touch with would be in Dubai soon. I was super excited that Adey was moving. But before she finally did, my dad visited.

My dad was the only man that called me "Baby" consistently, even though I may never understand why full-grown men and women call each other that. Maybe when I get to the stage where love makes me feel like a baby, I will relate.

He had started dropping hints and subtle pressure to settle down in our conversations.

"Give me the names of the guys asking you out so I can pray about it," he would say. My mum would have been the one to do this but ever since she passed, my dad incorporated the role of my mum into his swiftly. That was a beautiful gesture.

In the Nigerian society, it is not out of place for your parents to ask about who you are dating at a certain age

- even though they had chased all the men that you truly loved away when you were younger and told you to focus on your studies. This is a cultural norm that I cannot promise will stop in my generation. However, if I could, I would make sure the pressure to make a good and lasting impact in the world outweighs the pressure to be somebody's wife or husband.

And so, each time he tried to start that conversation, I told him about my larger-than-life plans and the steps I was taking to bring them to reality.

My dad was a funny man: he thought that I had quite exquisite taste, loved the finer things of life too much and catered to my lifestyle. He made it a point of duty to preach tithing and prudence to me every morning. He used to tell me to buy just one new cloth per month. How will a girl survive with just twelve clothes in her closet in a year?!

I loved him so much and his love for me helped me to better understand why God loves me even more. His visit refueled me for a few months and helped me cater to Adey's excesses when she finally arrived.

Adey brought out the crazy girl in me. We started partying a little and my social confidence level was charged back to a hundred percent. We all need friends like Adey who will laugh very deeply with you for hours unending, be your prayer partner, and hold you accountable for everything - and vice versa.

Starting in Dubai was a hard time for her as well. She experienced more hardship than I did in my own time, but she always found solace in dancing away her sorrows, so I had to always go out dancing with her.

One of the nights we had gone out partying, I met Tosin. Truth is, I can be anthropophobic when I choose to. What is there to not fear about human companionship, anyways? But that night was special. I had initially put on my introvert hat and even turned in the opposite direction, knowing full well that Tosin was coming in through the left door.

"Hi, guys." His voice sounded like he had just finished praising God with the angels in heaven, so I decided to loosen up a little bit and turned my head towards him.

Oh, sweet Lion of Zion! Tosin had to be the first man I had ever seen look so good in the dark - and his fragrance dispersed within seconds. I could smell wood, basil, leather, some musk, and a bit of vanilla afterward. Ah! It had to be *Amouage Memoir Man*. Tosin had a plan with this alluring and irresistible fragrance. Goodness! I could not think properly anymore.

The way his knees bent as he sat graciously next to me looked like he would be about 173cm tall - just right. His neatly trimmed silver goatee gave me a hint that he would be very mature - which made me smile considering all the immaturity I had had to deal with in the past years.

His eyes looked so good from the lens of his glasses - need I say more for a girl who looks good in glasses herself? I love men who wear glasses, it just makes them look intelligent and serious, even though that is usually not the case. I imagined he was in his early thirties - what more can a young woman approaching her thirties ask for?

My love for dark-skinned men came rushing back like the burst of energy that fills my niece up after she consumes a cup of ice cream. I had become color blind towards men when I met Fisayo four years ago. He had the best caramel skin I had ever seen - then he broke my heart, and I met Ademilola 'the light-skinned prince' who abused the purchase of designer brands. He made me forget 'dark-skinned men' completely and I started to dream about making light-skinned babies with thick black hair. Oh, my love for Yoruba men will forever remain undying even though they have been tagged demonic heart-wrenchers, "Yoruba demons" for short.

I looked away from Tosin after saying hello and for about five minutes, I could feel the silence on my chest. I had worn a low-neck dress that revealed half my twin bosom. The length of the dress had reduced further as I sat, so I constantly tried to pull it to reach my knee. I wondered if it were a good idea or not, whether he would judge me by my choice of 'unruly' dressing.

"How long have you lived in Dubai?" He finally broke my chain of restless thoughts.

"This is my third year now," I replied with my sweetest voice. I had learned the art of charming people with my voice a long time ago. I am not sure if it is a gift from God or something I picked up from movies but I had several people who admired me because of the sound of my voice.

Of course, it worked with Tosin. We talked and talked like lovers till we left the party. What bothered me a little was when we got talking about the Black Panther movie.

"It's more than a movie. It's the truth and I wish we had these superheroes for real," I had said passionately.

"Ryan Coogler did an amazing job with that one. My son went on and on about it a few days ago over the phone," he laughed as though laughing at my surprise. He had a son and is probably married. I rolled my eyes as I thought about it, but some part of me felt more relaxed. How many men will reveal this just like that - or maybe it just slipped from his mouth, who knows?

He asked me how old I was, and I paused for about ten seconds, then laughed: I wonder why women hesitate before telling their age. I have never been the type to hold back from revealing the supposed "secret of a lifetime". I hear it is solely because everything changes as soon as you hear a person's age, women especially. I agree - people begin to judge her appearance, assess her accomplishments, and, oh dear! Marriage!

I remember how a guy once asked my age when I was only nineteen, then said he would like to see me when I clocked twenty-six because he thought I would have "blossomed properly" by then. I did not take it personally though. I had always known I was a late bloomer, so whether the buttocks started to wiggle at age forty or fifty or never, it did not bother me.

So, I answered Tosin, "I'm three hundred and thirty-six months old."

He laughed so hard, and it made me smile. I like when people find me funny, weird, or different. It is like winning an award.

"Okay, I'll do the math. Wow, twenty-eight. You're pretty young."

"Oh, I'm not. Even though I'm still my father's baby, I know I'm hitting that dreaded year and losing the pretty number two soon."

He smiled, and the way his eyelids flickered made me smile back. We both pretended there was no connection, but honestly, I felt I had met my future husband.

"I moved back to Nigeria when I was thirty-one..." Wait. What?! I could not resist the urge to know his age, so I cut him short.

"So that was how many years ago?"

"I'm forty-six now".

I froze and became warm in seconds. Not only is this

man married, but he is also almost twice my age - and has a son, and maybe a daughter too.

I quickly snapped out of all my fantasies.

However, it was too late from his end. He had fallen in love with me. He kept sending me messages and wanted to see me again. I wanted to see him too, but how was I supposed to explain this one? Gosh!

When I told Adey about it, she was outraged.

"Not again! You have not sorted out your tangled romance with Femi, you want to bring in Tosin. Are you even in your right senses?" Adey glared deep into my eyes with a squint as if she could see my heart from a distance.

"Adey, look the heart doesn't choose whom it will love., it just goes on to love and that is not my fault ..."

"Ah, they've gotten you big time," she cut me short. "We have to put a leash on that heart so that your brain can function. You can't keep exposing your heart to all these *wahala* because it affects my own heart too. Please use your brain - I believe that one will choose for you."

"It's your mouth that needs a leash. Just keep quiet and

119

let me be. The day you leave Rashid - the father of three - alone, I will ask for your big-mouthed opinion, thank you."

She walked away quietly, and we went to bed with our hearts wanting the wrong men.

***

Sprawled on the sofa as usual after an exhausting workout session at the fitness club, I woke up from a dream, sighed, and picked up my phone to scroll through the conversation I had been having with Yinka.

We had met briefly on the metro when he got up for me to sit. I had wondered why he got up, seeing that I was neither pregnant nor old and wrinkled. I concluded he was just a sweet gentleman after I had gotten to my metro stop, and he did not follow me as most men would. He had the looks also, but the only thing we had exchanged that day was a smile.

"How long have you been behind me, silly?" I dropped my phone when I felt Adey's breathe on my neck.

"I see you're still bitter about your revelation," she spluttered with laughter. "Maybe you guys should just communicate in Yoruba if that makes you feel better. I

120

mean, he's the best guy for you - as of now; he has always treated you right since you guys met on the train; he has a great job; he is everything you prayed for, babe. Don't allow something as little as his intonation to tear you apart."

I looked at Adey with disgust and kept scrolling.

I had gone through a whirlwind romance with Yinka on my own, even before I knew his name. About a week after our train episode, fate brought us together again at another train station. This time, we exchanged pleasantries like old friends and exchanged numbers too.

We had been chatting on the phone for six months nonstop, until my birthday when he phoned. To my surprise, he had the most intense Yoruba intonation that shocked me. I had never heard someone speak English that sounded so much like Yoruba in my entire life.

"I'm more bothered about how it never occurred to me to call or visit him once over the six months we'd been chatting. I cannot deal God. I'll pass," I said as I looked up to the ceiling as though I could see God staring right back at me.

I concluded that I was done with men for good until my Prince Charming sweeps me off my feet, but until then, I tried to break some shells and lose some guard.

I went partying again. That night, the very versatile DJ had been giving us so much life with his blend of oldies, classics, and trendy playlist. He was the best thing that happened to that party after the booze. My friend and I were pretty much "mo gbọ mo ya" (uninvited guests) who acted like we were invited. We even sat at the most active table. I had danced and rocked myself so much - and hadn't the slightest idea that a man old enough to birth me twice was falling head over heels for me. This was a party where almost all the older men had their eyes fixed on our table for some reason, even with their wives right beside them.

After some time, our mutual friend on whose ticket we had attended the party came telling me that a couple of her older male friends had their eyes on me and would like to talk. I did not understand what that meant at first. I had thought they were just passing comments and, honestly, I am not even the type of girl to be noticed at parties because, as much as I try to have fun, I do it conservatively. I create boundaries for myself where everything starts and ends, so I paid no attention to the talk.

Surprisingly, in less than ten minutes, one of them had gotten a little chance to get away from his wife's radar. He walked straight to our table and said hello to everyone without looking suspicious. At this time, I had forgotten the discussion I had with our mutual friend, so I felt he was just a random man trying to have fun on the coolest table. Then he grabbed a glass, sat next to me and the conversation started. He introduced himself as Tade and said I could call him "T" for short.

He had tinted glasses on at night, so I could not see his eyes to decipher how he looked at me. He wore a black tuxedo because the party was a black-tie event, so he appeared decent and I could not tell what was about to happen.

He tried striking a conversation with me. At this time, I was not even aware that his wife was nearby. I was a million percent innocent with him all through and acted as normal as I was. He excused himself midway into our conversation and said he would be right back - and I remember not giving a damn whether he came back or not because I did not attend the party to talk to random men. I hate having random conversations that will lead me nowhere great. I only later realized that he left because he had noticed that his wife was staring at him.

The photographer had fallen head over heels with my friends and I and our look and had suggested that we meet him outside the ballroom for a brief photoshoot, which we agreed to. Mr. T had now seen the biggest opportunity to talk some more, and so he followed our trail out the ballroom, a few minutes later.

It was then I saw him clean and clear. He was no different from those thirsty old men who would randomly park their Range Rovers by your side as you walk on the road and catcall. He did not even mince words at all - probably because he had little time to make his intentions known before someone came nagging.

He told me how beautiful I looked and how I had captured his attention. As a form of respect which I really would not accord to a younger man, I smiled back at him and told him, "Thank you," then went ahead to dial my number on his phone.

I thought, "He'll be going back to London tomorrow, and I'm pretty sure he's a busy businessman who might not call me, or be bothered if I don't answer his calls after the first time. So, there's nothing to lose." He was the most excited man that night after he saved my number and dashed back to his wife's side.

The party went on and my friends and I partied like there was no other person in the room but us. The only thing I noticed was the fact that the booze kept coming and Adey kept drinking. While I rested for a moment, Mr. T's wife was getting ready to go to bed and was doing her last chitchats for the night from table to table. When she got to ours, she had the sweetest voice. She pleasantly hugged everyone, including me - and that just stuck. I could not get myself to hurt her even if I had had the intentions. She stayed longer at our table as though she intentionally wanted to pass a silent message across to me.

When we finally decided that we had had enough, we stepped out into our other friend's hotel room to put ourselves together and catch our breaths before heading home. Suddenly, the bell rang and, behold, it was Mr. T and his friends.

125

I cannot remember what irritated me more - the fact that Adey was now so tipsy that she kept falling, or the fact that we were in a room with three older men whose wives were just downstairs.

I was so reluctant to talk to Mr. T. He asked at some point why I was running away from him, and I lied that I had to pick up something from the far end of the room. He sure knew I was not that type of girl, but he still gave it a try: he started to talk about things that would interest me like my career, future, and other important things.

He showed more interest after he realized he had been able to make me comfortable with him, and went on to tell me how he could make my life easier and better, and how our friendship could elevate me and make my dreams come true.

For a moment, I was happy. I felt my financial troubles were about to be over because God had indeed blessed me with Mr. T.

He went on to proudly delve into details about his IT company which takes him all over the world - and this got me drooling internally at the thought of money.

The talk was beginning to get boring when he took my right hand and started to caress it slowly. That act would normally turn me on immediately if I was with someone I loved, but I became self-conscious because of my cracked nail polish instead and immediately withdrew my hand back from him courteously with a smile.

He noticed and said it was okay, that he was not trying to do anything silly - and he picked it again and continued. He must have thought I was the naivest girl on earth since I had not slapped him yet.

Soon, I had had enough of all the absurdities of the night, especially with my drunk friend constantly saying crazy things like, "Why does the toilet look different?" That was my cue to get up and get us home before the horny men took advantage of her state.

And as though Mr. T had been planning it since the first time, he set his eyes on me, he did not even wait for me to say goodbye: he planted the slimiest kiss on my lips that set my brain back to normal in a split second. He kept pushing his tongue into my mouth as if there was something on it that he wanted me to swallow.

That must go down in history as the most disgusting kiss of all time.

As much as I had thought he had been too forward for himself, I believed that kiss was another prompt to run for my dear life. We got into the taxi and headed straight home, and the first thing I did was block his number from reaching me before he even tried. I might have lost the fastest luxury lifestyle that came on a platter of gold, but I needed my dignity intact - especially because I had just only recently started to understand my purpose in life.

The next day did not get better because of my decision, but my heart felt a type of peace that no amount of money could buy.

That experience reminded me of when my cousin tried to sleep with me. Just like Mr. T, Ife was quite bouyant financially. He had told me to meet him up somewhere as he was returning from a trip, and I had trusted that because he was family, I was safe. It was not until he planted a sloppy kiss on my lips that I realized that I was not safe. He pulled at me, whispered sweet rubbish that made my left ear tingle and itchy, and tried to put me in the mood but I just was not having it. So, I withdrew to a corner until morning.

After that day, I never collected anything from him because I felt he was only trying to buy me over for sex - and I became uninterested in older men.

These experiences however never changed my sexual orientation or my love for men generally. Good men are always pleasing to my discerning heart and Yoruba men still get the award for best men category. Period!

WHAT'S BETTER THAN GOLD?

"Your life is worth much more than Gold."

Bob Marley

Peace of mind. That is what I consider better than Gold and, in all honesty, peace of mind is more spiritual than intangible. Dubai offers some measure of peace and comfort. If there is anywhere you will ever go and not worry about forgetting something in a taxi or at the table of your favorite outdoor restaurant, because you love their seafood so much, you just had to forget yourself, it is Dubai, but just make sure you report it because your lost items will not suddenly come back to you miraculously.

We once forgot a bride's traditional wedding outfit that cost a fortune in the trunk of a taxi that drove about 40 minutes from Sharjah down to Dubai. Unfortunately, her wedding was a few hours away and she had to focus on enjoying the day. She was unable to wear the outfit for her wedding but she still got it back some days after. Thousands of Dirhams have been retrieved from taxi drivers by riders who forgot to exit with their luggage.

Adey also forgot her purse one time on the train, when she went shopping at the gold market. She immediately reported to the RTA staff at the Rashidya metro station and after a few phone calls, her purse was returned to her in one piece. Meanwhile in some other cities, retrieving your lost items will come at a cost or without an assurance that you will eventually get it back.

If you equally forget something you had purchased in the market, there is a chance you will find it.

The gold market in Deira, popularly known as Gold Souq, is the next best thing to peace of mind, according to Adey. That place is Adey's favorite place in Dubai – not mine though. If you want to get the purest 18 to 24 karat gold and you visit the gold and diamond park just by the Umm Al Sheif Metro Station and you do not find what you like, make sure you go to Gold Souq in Deira. Although, going gold shopping is not my favorite thing to do in Dubai, I love that buying gold is still considerably cheaper in Dubai compared to other countries in the world and all gold merchants sell at the same rate because merchandise sold by jewelers is regulated by the Dubai government, ensuring the authenticity of any gold item sold. You can negotiate the charges that applies for making the ornament. Making charges vary depending on the type of gold jewelry you want to buy and the retailer you are buying from. While bargaining is somewhat challenging in bigger jewelry stores in the mall, you will not have the same concern in the shops in the Souq. Depending on the gold price in Dubai and the amount you are purchasing, you can bring the making charges down to a significantly low amount.

Even better, tourists can claim VAT refunds in the UAE for all purchases made in the country - the joy of holding on to all shopping receipts.

If you enjoy history, fashion, or just love the idea of being surrounded by tons of gold in different shapes and sizes, then you should never miss Dubai Gold Souq. The first time I visited the Souq, I was smitten. Just before the entrance, I marveled at how the visual merchandisers of these roadside gold shops displayed their merchandise, from impossibly heavy necklaces to actual dresses. You will desire to own a piece and if you cannot afford a piece, you will save some money till you can get a piece.

If you have seen any viral video of Pakistani merchants speaking Nigerian languages, you will find those guys in Deira Market. When you visit Dubai as a Nigerian, and you do not visit the Deira market then something is wrong. Nigerians and Deira market are like five and six. I don't know what annoys me more about the market - the fact that getting there can be confusing if you go there after a long time with the train switches at the red and green line intersections or the fact that the actual market requires a lot of walking, and you could get lost if you missed your way. The good thing however is that, if you want to start a good business, Deira is your go-to place. Before getting a job, I had invested some of my savings in a handbag business. It was very lucrative that I helped a few of my friends start their small business from this market and I got so used to products from Dubai that if I was anywhere else and I saw a shoe or handbag, I would know it was purchased from Dubai. Things are cheaper in the market and that's where you will find everything, from local restaurants to textile and fabric, to food and spices merchants.

The wholesale plaza houses a lot of merchants who sell all sorts of merchandise at wholesale price. Whatever it is you want to buy, Deira is the place to find it at a cheaper rate. So next time you visit Dubai, adorn yourself with gold and some peace of mind.

THIS SKIN COLOR AGAIN

"I have a dream that my four little children will one day live in a nation where they will not be judged by the color of their skin, but by the content of their character".

Martin Luther King, Jr.

I wailed and wept because I could not take it anymore. My skin color had betrayed me once again. She had warned them, but they did not listen, and so, when she saw me, she thought I was one of them and burst into a rage. She did not listen to me or notice my surprise.

"I told all three of you never to use my stuff again." She kept on yelling, and I kept repeating, "Me? Me? Did you tell me? Me?"

I did not need a psychic to tell me I had been mistaken for my fellow black sisters, even though we looked different to an extent, our hair was braided to the back the same way, and our accent sort of sounded the same - so I was taking the blow for their sins.

Every day, I try to live a peaceful life. In my country, they say, "Jeje ọmọ Eko mi n lọ." I do not make trouble and I flee from the same so I try to live with different kinds of humans.

However, the day I was mistaken for one of the other girls that lived in the first room by the door of my flat, I lost my peace. I was at war with myself, my identity, my color, my race, and everything.

Three black girls had moved into my flat a month after the Egyptian sisters went back to their country for Ramadan. Immediately they moved in, I could already discern a high level of discomfort in an apartment I had managed to live in for a little over four months.

All three of them are light-skinned, and that made me notice the thick black hairs on the legs of one of them. She is so hairy; one can braid on it. Another had blue hair, and the third was very smiley. She will say "hi" and "bye" every time she saw me. They all smoked drank alcohol and spoke at the top of their voices every night. They slept during the day and were always up all night mainly because they worked at night. Whatever that meant, I did not care because our paths barely crossed - and that was fine.

One night, we were all asleep, and, for the first time in my entire life, the fire alarm woke me up from deep sleep due to the smoke detection - it was not a drill. The building security had to come up to our flat to warn the girls, who had been smoking all night in their little balcony.

I had no idea the Russian girl in the second room had previously had an altercation with the girls because they always used her things and never cleaned up. We were flatmates, and we shared each other's kitchen utensils sometimes, but these girls were extremely dirty.

Now, here I was, living a quiet life and using the same thing I had used for the past few months - and she kept pointing her index finger at me, warning me never to touch her wok pan ever again.

Did I use her wok pan? Yes. But had she ever told me not to? No.

I was scared for my life. I had never seen a Russian get angry. I had only heard about their fierceness from my former Ukrainian flatmate who never liked to be referred to as a Russian for many reasons and changed her Emirati boyfriends like she was changing underwear - but that is by the way.

I was hurt. I wanted the floor to swallow me up quickly or do something else to take that experience away because I could not explain at that time that I had been mistaken for someone else.

The sudden rage was unstoppable. She needed to vent,

and I had to listen, regardless of whether I pleaded guilty or not. When she was done, she walked away feeling undefeated.

I was lost. My thought chain was shattered into incomprehensible pieces.

The next minute, her roommate came to apologize to me for the mix-up. I stood still in the kitchen, voiceless, broken, and hurt. I think the apology hurt more than the accusation. I suddenly burst into quiet hot tears. I had finally been vindicated but it did not take the shame away. Neither did it transfer all her words to the actual people it was meant for.

What sort of thing is that? How can someone mix people up, and then cause so much difficulty, confusion, and pain in just a matter of minutes?

Unfair right? Exactly! Unfair is the life that we have come to live in this black skin. No matter where you go, the only place you do not see how different your color makes you is in your home country, with your family.

I was done in the kitchen. I walked into my room, already overwhelmed at noon. I thought about how I have had to step aside a few times at major bus stops or metro stations just to present my ID for a check; how it took more than a year of back and forth to different banks before I knew I would never be able to open a bank account; how I was never able to live in an apartment I loved so much; how empty taxis did not stop for me and how I had to wait for longer than normal before I got a taxi; how white men stopped their cars and rolled down their windows to utter silly remarks as I walked on the roadside.

All of these and more because some people with my skin color had messed up in the past and are probably still messing up - and I would have to grow up living on the edge.

That is an unfair situation to live in.

YAHOO GIRLS

"Rather fail with honor than succeed by fraud".

SOPHOCLES

I was in our shared kitchen that day when I saw someone walk in and out. She looked just like me, young, dark-skinned, pretty, but she looked unhappy. She walked in a second time to dump some bowls in the kitchen sink and walked away again. I rolled my eyes and thought "Ugh, she's just like them - untidy and annoying."

This new girl came from the room opposite mine, where three other Nigerian girls lived, and made all the noise that could have come from two nurseries put together. We could not tell whether they were fighting or having fun most of the time. We only knew they were awake when we slept, and they were asleep whenever we left for work. Our paths barely crossed on weekdays.

On that day, a weekend, the young lady walked in the third time and this time she said hi. For a moment I thought someone else was there with us until she moved closer to me and said, "I'm greeting you."

"Oh, hi." I forced a smile, and just when I thought that was all we had to say to each other, she asked if there was a vacancy at my office.

"Oh. I'm sorry there's no vacancy right now," I said shaking my head with a sad look on my face.

I could feel her disappointment in my stomach. I felt I had to give her some hope, so I went on to tell her about a sister-friend who was pregnant and in need of help. She looked up for a minute as though she was seeking counsel from the ceiling and then looked back at me, smiled, and said, "Please I don't mind."

By this time, I had finished cooking my two-minute noodles, so I told her I had to go eat and would get back to her later. We exchanged numbers and I went into my room.

For some uncanny reason, I was eager to help so I sent a message to my friend who truly discussed needing a maid with me, and immediately, we started negotiating payments and working hours with her. This activity alone was about a weeklong. I learned during that week that Juliet was twenty years old even though she looked twice my age and was more desperate for a job than I thought.

She had sent me a message that week saying that she

needed to see me urgently. Eager to know what the situation was, I ran out and saw her sitting outside the door like a bereaved wife.

"Is everything okay?" I asked as I moved closer to her.

"Everything no dey okay o. Nothing is okay." She repeated this like three times and got me more concerned. I gave her some time to muster all the courage she needed to spill the beans because she kept watching the door to be sure no one was coming out.

"Hmmn, my sister, I'm not okay. I want to either go back home or get this job," she finally spoke in hushed tones. "Please don't tell anyone what I am about to tell you and don't tell anyone that I am looking for a job, please."

"Okay, fantastic. What's the problem?"

"I was introduced to my boss by my yellow friend."

She described another girl in the room - curvy with thoroughly bleached skin, who happened to be her childhood friend. She had been told by this yellow friend that life was easy, that all the grasses in Dubai were green, and that jobs were flowing like milk and honey on the streets of Dubai and all she had to do was agree to a few terms and she will be made forever. She agreed to get sponsorship from her yellow friend's boss who paid for an international passport, a three-month UAE visa, and a return ticket.

It was not until she got to Dubai that she realized that she could not do that sort of job.

"He go call us for any time of the night make we dress up and prepare to meet up with a client." She switched from pidgin English to proper English in every sentence.

Their boss was a virtual pimp who lived and schooled in Malaysia as Juliet had confirmed and he had different platforms where he hooked up randy men from all walks of life with girls like Juliet. He will send pictures to these men or clients as they call them, and they will select and agree on a certain price, date, time, and venue. This was prostitution but the flip side to it was that the pictures their boss sends are always different from the real humans who must show up at the location. So, it is a catfish situation literally.

Now, here is the real job: to fight for payment - whether

the clients liked what they saw or not.

The client will become displeased that they have been catfished and says, "No, you are not the person I saw in the picture, leave," and the girls will say, "I don't care. I am not leaving here without my payment."

There will eventually be a fight, and because the client will not involve the police due to the sensitivity of the case in such a city as Dubai, they either pay up - or both parties hurt each other while the girl insists on payment.

So, on a few occasions, the client willingly makes payment to avoid further complications, but more often, it leads to a fight and the girl would forcefully take her payment after struggling and receiving the beating of her life. Bottom line is, she can never leave the client without getting some money off him to pay the boss.

"I don tire to dey chop blow. My whole body dey pain me because these men dey beat me well well and I no sabi fight - so I dey always run commot without getting paid. I just wan dey go back Nigeria. I no do again and my boss dey disturb me for money."

At that point, I had so many questions to ask. I was not

146

sure what to describe that sort of job as - it was not exactly prostitution, neither was it stealing, but it seemed closer to being described as fraud.

After she told me the story, I remember inviting her to my church. As far as I was concerned, only Jesus could help her out as I had no clue what to do to help. The job I was trying to get her had to be put on hold because I had to watch my back as well as my friend's.

I also advised her to forfeit her return ticket, which was two months away, book a new one as soon as she could, to reunite with her family. She took my advice, was able to raise some funds, and fled for her dear life.

After recounting the story to my friend, she said she had heard of similar stories - and that those kinds of girls are called *Yahoo Girls*.

THE INCOMPLETE ABORTION

"I can be changed by what happens to me. But I refuse to be reduced by it."

Maya Angelou

H ello, I need to talk to you about something.

The message came into my phone at a quarter past midnight, but I was in deep sleep and did not see the message until I woke up in the morning six hours after.

"Are you okay?"

"Can I call you?"

I replied immediately because it was strange for him to send a message like that. We were quite close, and he managed to trust me with certain things as a teenager, and even though I always struggle with being overly critical of people, (which sometimes makes me distant), I still tried to be there for him as much as I could.

However, that morning was different. I knew he needed me, and I had to help. I became very anxious to know what the matter could be.

I got out of bed to get ready for work, hoping that he would have replied before I got back from the bathroom. Thirty minutes went by and I had gotten no response. I dialed his number repeatedly as I sat on my dressing table. The day was getting brighter and brighter and I had to leave for work, so I said a short prayer for him and did the only thing I could do at that moment: Wait.

A few minutes into my trip to work, I heard my phone beep. As I waited to get on the bus, I read his message: "I don't know how to put it, but all I know is that my girlfriend has just missed her period."

The first thing I did was laugh and heave a sigh of relief. I laughed because it was not a life-or-death situation as I imagined. I also found it a bit funny. I never knew he was sexually active, and I never imagined I would one day have that conversation with him or with anyone at that.

It seems like a part of our culture to just dabble into the sex situation on our own and figure it all out till we end up lucky enough to survive all our mistakes or fall pregnant "outside wedlock", or worse.

It was unbelievable, but since it was the 9th of April, it did not pass for an "April fool" prank. I laughed again because I had been so worried. I did not even realize the seriousness until another text message came in:

"I don't want to father a child at the age of twenty."
"You're twenty?" I replied almost immediately. "Why

are you having unprotected sex at twenty?"

I was not sure if that was the right question to throw at him, but I was getting agitated because it had just occurred to me that he was serious, and we needed to figure out what to do next.

He became very worried about my questions. I had never confirmed "positive" to a pregnancy test before, so I did not understand what he or his girlfriend were going through at the time. I tried hard not to throw my opinions on him, so I told him I needed to confirm what they could do from a friend and get back to him.

As soon as I got on the bus and found a seat, I searched for Grace's number and asked for counsel. Grace always knows what to do and is very wise with her advice. She however did not sound cheerful. She sounded even more pensive as she spoke and asked me if they used contraceptives and if they had confirmed with PT strips. She told me to confirm from him and said she needed to hurry somewhere, but I was so concerned about my twenty-year-old young cousin to have caught what was wrong with Grace.

I sent him messages till I got to work and encouraged him to stay positive because he had gotten to the point where he was sure God was angry with him as he recounted his previous abortions. I said a little prayer for him and got on with work. I also told him to give me feedback after a few days while I wondered why people wasted so much time feeling God was angry with them instead of focusing on God's kindness and love.

Eventually, after a few days, he shared with me that her period came flowing like a river - and this was where I was happy to unleash my well of opinions from where I had tethered them all along:

"Condoms are not that expensive, neither are contraceptives - and abstinence will help you become more responsible. All three will save you from errors and mistakes. Choose one and be wise because there is so much more beauty in life than dealing with the consequences of some minutes' pleasure at this age."

I had not been that candid in a long time, and I was happy I could help him make better decisions in the future. My only hope was that he would act on my advice.

A few weeks after, Grace came over to mine and told me she needed to tell me something.

"With what I'm about to tell you, Busola, I know you will be disappointed - but I don't want you judging me."

I started to smile because when people start to talk like that, it always sounds like they are about to crack a dry joke or prank me.

She looked at me for another minute, contemplating whether to tell me or not, then plunged in.

"When my ex came visiting two months ago…" she smiled, reminding me to keep a neutral look as she noticed I was already giving her the repellant look when she said "ex".

I fixed my face and gave a deep sigh even though I did not know where it was going.

"I went visiting Ken in the hotel apartment where he lodged, and we talked for a while." She paused again and at that point, I smiled because I felt it had to be something good.

"Things happened, Busola, and I got pregnant," she finally said, then looked away.

Apparently, when I called Grace to seek her counsel for my young cousin, she was also dealing with a similar situation.

I felt cold shivers on my face. The look I gave her at this point was as though she had spat on me. I went mum for what seemed like hours till she looked back at me, and I straightened my face again.

"Grace! Why didn't you use protection?" Again, I was asking the wrong question.

"It's a little too late to ask that question now, Busola. I have removed the fetus and I am no longer pregnant."

"What?!" I pressed my palms on both sides of my cheek and opened my mouth in disbelief as I gave out a loud sigh.

"Yes. The only reason I am telling you this now is because the fetus was not completely drained out."

"No way!" My voice suddenly became baritone.

"I am sick, Busola. I don't know what will happen to me. A Kenyan nurse injected a medication in me to help with the removal. I bled for days unending and for the past two months, I have not stopped bleeding."

"We need to get you to the hospital, fast!" I started getting uneasy.

"No, Busola, we cannot go to the hospital. What if they called the police on me?"

I suddenly remembered the law. How detrimental and illegal it was for any woman who is unmarried or single, to fall pregnant while residing in UAE. The consequences of local authorities discovering that any unmarried woman is carrying a baby can include jail and deportation. If we had gone to a specialist hospital for evacuation and treatment, we might have never returned home.

I felt sick and helpless all over again. We did not know what to do, but we finally thought of travelling to a farther, cheaper, and more lenient emirate to see a doctor. We had to lie that she was married and had had a sudden miscarriage even before they asked for details.

Luckily for us, she was not asked for any proof. She got treated and got better soon enough.

Thankfully, these laws have now been relaxed. I certainly do not see why removing a fetus should be illegal. No woman should be punished for not wanting to grow a fetus inside of her. It should be up to her as much as it is up to any adult to make life decisions for themselves.

DETTY DECEMBER

"When one door closes another door opens; but we so often look so long and so regretfully upon the closed door, that we do not see the ones which open for us".

Alexander Graham Bell

It was my last December in Dubai. I had butterflies in my stomach every waking moment. I was in love and happy to finally be able to give all the love in me to someone. It felt like the right time. I just had to love him, and I went the entire length of loving someone I barely knew, again. This was a sign that I had healed from my previous hurt, or maybe not.

I had never travelled without telling someone from my family. One person at least had to know that I would be stuck in the air for up to seven hours and expect the laws of gravity to happen at the estimated time also. However, this Christmas, I decided to fly home to the love of my life without informing my family.

It was very unlike me to make such a drastic decision and, for someone who is exceptionally indecisive, flying home to a young man was the riskiest thing to do. But I did it anyway and thought I would surprise my dad and siblings on New Year's Eve.

Sayo had typed "Hello, Busola" in my DM in January, two years before. I never enjoyed receiving messages from random people on social media. I was not doing any business whatsoever on my page, so I did not always expect random hellos because I honestly do not make friends easily and I enjoy my own company a little too much - so new people always made me panic.

The interesting thing about Sayo was that his page was private so I could not tell what he looked like unless I followed him. I got curious. I wanted to know who it was, what he had to say, and how he had the nerve to put my name after the "Hello," but I did not want to request to follow him. Very typical of me.

So, I merely replied, "Hello." I would have also inserted his name just after the hello, but his ID did not look like a name and his display photo was in black and white.

I got a response almost immediately. "How are you today? I'm sure you're wondering who this is, right?" I raised an eyebrow and thought, "Well, you are damn right, mister."

"I'm doing well, thanks - I'm just thinking you must know me from somewhere," I replied to him with a blank stare emoji.

Quite frankly, the conversation was getting too long as far as I was concerned. We had no mutual friends and it just made me more curious.

After a few minutes of nonstop chatting, I decided to click

the request button - and there he was: that 72% cacao that was missing in my chocolate.

I scrolled from photo to photo, and I yearned to know more. He was courteous, attentive, and he looked good from his photos. So, I decided to keep this one even though he had seemed a little bit disappointed that we were miles apart.

I got to Lagos, Nigeria at about 4 p.m. WAT on boxing day. A little disagreement had sprung up regarding airport transfers - I wanted him to pick me up by himself for no special reason other than that it just felt special, but he wanted to send a driver over instead. There had not been a time I flew into Lagos and Daddy was not waiting at the airport, so Sayo had to forgive me for wanting him to do the pick-up even if that was the only time, he would ever have to do it.

He agreed to it last minute and I sort of felt bad that I stressed him out, especially because he was busy at work - but I still felt special anyways. If there was a lesson to learn from that, it was never to enforce your needs on anyone if you are not paying for it, especially if it is because you are used to that need being met in a certain way. We should all learn to ease into new people gently.

The ride to his home was a bit awkward. I was oddly shy, and I did not know if I was doing the right thing. I had no expectations, but I just prayed the holidays would be the best decision I had ever made. So much hope for a "*Detty December*". I had informed only two of my friends about the trip just so I could hang out with other people at some point during the trip, even though my family had no idea I was a few minutes away from them.

Sayo was no longer a stranger from the internet during this trip. I had seen Sayo a few times before that Boxing Day. The first time we ever saw each other, I had visited my family briefly and decided to set up a date with him. I wore a long, flared, African-print skirt and a button-up sweater. My hair had been tightly braided in a color that did not look great with my skin tone, my sandals had broken while I hustled to get on a bus and made a little noise as I walked, and I had carried a backpack because I do not travel with handbags in my suitcase. In a nutshell, I did not put my best foot forward.

My siblings and I had gone to church to pray that morning and I had had to dress up for church. I knew I might have underdressed for a first date, but I did not think much about it. I was early and had met with another friend for a quick drink, and we talked nonstop till Sayo showed up. We had lunch and were together for about a little over two hours. I remember how it was my first-time eating quesadillas in Lagos and enjoyed it.

He told me about how he lost his dad over a decade ago and his mum five years after he lost his dad. He told me how the loss moved him closer to God and how his story had been God all the way. He looked too good for anyone to believe he had hawked food when he was much younger just to support his mum. He adored her from all his stories. He had also mentioned that he would like to marry a woman like his mum - a woman who always raised her husband in prayer - that stuck with me and even though I felt like that was a good thing to desire, I also felt that it would be better if he was a bit more open-minded.

He had also visited me once in Dubai and that was the most exciting feeling ever. I had always pressured him to stop over on my side of the world whenever he travelled, and he did on a business trip to India. He had stopped by for forty-eight hours at a time my dad was also visiting Dubai. My attention, time, and money were a major concern, but the joy outweighed the worry. We talked, shopped, and got to know each other a little bit more in a little time. It was a tad overwhelming to shuttle between my dad's hotel and his hotel in that short time, but it was well worth it - and that was the beginning of the actual butterflies that now led to my *Detty December* with Sayo.

We drove to VGC where he lived with his brother who was out of town that period. From the parking lot, he offloaded my heavy suitcase from the trunk and led me up to the second floor. I felt good - but not quite. A part of me just was not entirely comfortable, but again I did not give room to the negativity or whatever the feeling was.

He opened the giant door to the very clean and organized three-bedroom apartment I had always seen on our video calls and wheeled my suitcase to the bedroom. It was even more beautiful than I had seen on our calls, and I was so impressed with all he had done to his home. I finally got a big hug, and a little kiss was planted on my lips. Then he left me to freshen up while he ordered dinner.

I could not believe myself! I was on the moon, and all I saw were beautiful, love-shaped stars. I forgot there was a thing as jet lag and how much it messes me up after a few days of flying.

After I changed into shorts and a tank top for comfort, I stepped out to find him seated on the couch, watching

TV. He smiled and I smiled back. I sat next to him, constantly stealing glances at him and, within seconds, we were cuddled up. His warmth was different, he was gentle, and I could feel the genuineness in his touch.

His heart was also racing. I could sense his insecurity. He had welcomed a near-stranger into his home but being in cloud 9, both our brains had shut down. Soon, there was a knock on the door for delivery and we had seafood pasta, watched some more TV, and slept.

He slept but I kept tossing and turning. Sleeping anywhere new can be a headache sometimes and coupled with the jet lag, I almost got sick, so I kept trying till I was able to shut my eyes for a few minutes - and almost immediately, it was morning.

I got into the bathroom and stared blankly into the mirror for a few minutes. I blinked when I saw how badly I had physically prepared for the trip, so I decided to go to the salon for a few hours. He was busy in his study anyways and that would not be a problem, I thought.

He did not look very happy about me going out, but I promised him I would be back soon. He stayed working from home all day and as soon as I got back home, he made us lunch. We ate and he went back to work, then, in the evening, we stepped out for a short and quiet dinner.

For some reason, I was not enjoying his company as much as I thought I would and I believe the feeling was mutual because he was sort of withdrawn, unlike the day I got into town. At this point, I started to feel a little left out, so I arranged a day out with my friend for the next day and another friend for the day after, just so I could respect his space and his busy schedule. It suddenly started to feel like we were together but far apart. My mistake here was, noticing something and not communicating the same immediately. He kept his distance while I *dettied* Lagos and as I left him to go surprise my family for the New Year, he continued to keep mute.

My dad was the happiest to see me. He was surprised and kept asking how I managed to make a trip without letting him know. I handed him his Christmas present – more like a keep quiet gift so that he would not question my audacity any further, and he blessed me, got dressed, and went on to hang out with his friends. My little nieces were in awe, my siblings were full of joy, and I was overjoyed.

It must be the best feeling ever-surprising, loved ones with your presence during the holidays. Everyone should experience a joyful surprise in their lifetime. It's therapeutic.

We talked and laughed and talked again, and time went by so quickly - and soon, it was time to return to Sayo who had not spoken with me for about three days.

He had said he needed some time alone as he always liked to be alone at the end of the year to commune with God. He had that habit of just disappearing anyway - so it was okay if disappearing this time was to spend some quiet time with God. My luggage was still at his and I would leave for the airport from there, so I had to let him know I was on my way back.

"Hi, Sayo. I'm on my way back and I'm coming with some food for dinner."

"Okay, I'm in a meeting. See you soon."

It was obvious that things had changed and the butterflies were slowly dying, but I had no idea how to feed them to bring them back to life. I tried everything I could, but they stayed sick. I was deeply hurt, sad, and broken. What changed? It happened so fast and more so during a trip, we had both looked forward to for so long. I knew he found it hard to tell me what was wrong and I found it hard to reach him, but all I could do was pray. I prayed until I did not know what to say anymore - but nothing changed.

"Don't question him, don't feel bad, just talk to him normally, be nice and pray about it," my sister had advised.

So, I stayed cool, pressed on the doorbell, and there he was in a second, looking straight at me. I could see the joy in his eyes but masked with a blank look on his face. He looked at me like he would tear me apart if he said a word, and like he had so much to say but held back.

I hugged him and rolled my mini hand luggage in. I said hello to his guest, went straight into the room with my hands full of little bags, and got into the shower with a heavy heart. As the warm water from the shower trickled down my body, all I could do was wonder what had happened. My expectations had been cut into pieces, I was broken and had no idea what would happen next.

My flight was the next morning and if I could do anything, I had just a few hours to make it right - but the miracle never came. We slept, woke, had breakfast, and he was quiet except for when he had to answer phone calls. At some point, I tried to have the conversation, but he avoided it, so I was aware that he understood what he was doing. He remained on the phone for as long as he wanted and that prevented me from salvaging the situation.

I was sore inside. I felt like my organs were failing me and all I could do was breathe till it was time for him to leave home. Then he gave me a big hug and left me in his house for a meeting at work. I had to shut the door behind me and leave. I looked around, picked up my luggage and what was left of my heart, and headed to the airport with a confused heart and soul.

They say the price of love is loss. Well, that was a specially *detty* loss.

DADDY

*Praise be to the God and Father of our Lord Jesus Christ, the
Father of compassion and the God of all comfort, who comforts us in
all our troubles so that we can comfort those in any trouble with the
comfort we ourselves receive from God.*

2nd Corinthians 1:3 - 4 (NIV)

It was almost 10 p.m. on July 10 when my phone rang - my favorite person in the whole wide world was on the other end of the line. Moving back to Nigeria to be with family was the best decision I ever made since leaving Nigeria. While many people felt it was a bad idea, I had never been more convinced about anything. I spent so much quality time with my best guy – Just me and him.

"Ekaale o," I said happily as I had not spoken to him in two days. I had been away from him for two weeks, but we made it a point of duty to talk every day. So, missing two days was a lot, we had to catch up on everything that happened. He told me about his heart palpitation the day before and how it seemed very different from what he had always experienced. We tried to catch up on a few things and agreed to see the next day so that we could sleep early.

I was only about an hour into sleep when my phone started vibrating nonstop. It was my sister. "His heart palpitation has started again. Just pray for him."

It was already past midnight and very unsafe to go out to meet them. So, I stayed still in bed at my other sister's house. I could barely say a word of prayer. The night suddenly became darker than usual, and fear was looming around. I was not sure if it was fear I needed to bind or if I should just plead for help from God.

I knew how long the palpitations lasted, so I waited a few minutes before calling my sister back. "Busola, he's gone," she said softly, her voice shaking after every word.

"Okay...okay...okay". I could not say anything else.

My heart froze, the atmosphere changed and all I wanted to do was see my daddy, but I could not.

Death is ugly. It creeps in on you even when you feel like you are prepared for it.

The next time I saw him, his body laid still in the white *Buba, Sokoto, agbada* and shoes I had specially picked out for him. "He looks like he's just sleeping," I remember whispering to one of my sisters who nodded in agreement.

I lived in denial for a long time even after his funeral - and it took quite a while to figure things out. With grief, we were not trying to go back to how things were before. Rather, my siblings and I had a whole new life to create without our dad. Knowing that it was barely five years without our mum, it had to be a new process of healing forward.

He was an exceptional man with a heart full of love. He had so much love to spread around and always had an interest in peacemaking. He was the standard I had for a partner because I did not know a better man than he. He sacrificed for his family, gave, continued to give to non-family, and treated everybody equally. He used to say, "Busola, ma mu ọkọ ta ma ra shirt fun wa si le o" – "Busola do not bring a broke man home".

My dad gave to people like he had a vault that would never go empty. One day, I saw his account balance and I wondered how he managed to do it. He was a cheerful giver who sponsored several non-biological children to school. He took the responsibility of being a father and grandfather, to those who had no father figure. I shared my father with domestic staff, neighbors, and friends - yet I did not feel deprived because there was so much love to go around everybody, and it was just so easy to love him dearly.

I had been able to grieve my mum when she died because I had my dad, siblings, friends, and a very loving partner at the time, who all helped during the healing process. However, grieving daddy was like I had just lost everything and a little more, all over again – I felt "naked".

It was the most challenging moment of my life. I had a hard time sleeping for several months and yearned for a deep and genuine explanation of what was happening.

There was a huge disparity in the way my siblings and I grieved, and it was unsettling to always think that his death had hit me the most. We all grieved differently because we all had different relationships with him and more so because we all experience pain differently, but we still found solace in the unity and bond we shared. His grandchildren were very distraught and confused. They just saw him the previous day, dancing. How do you explain to little children who ask the same questions daily? It was tough.

People left, friends could not help for too long, and to top it all, there was a global pandemic. For the longest time, I asked why it had to be me who needed to go through all that pain of bereavement alone. I was afraid, lost in all sense, and most times I did not understand why I still needed to be alive.

My heart was removed far from my body, beating alone in an especially cold and unfamiliar place. It was unstable for days and I remember hating church, the Bible, and everything that had to do with faith and prayers all over again. I found solace in doing the wrong things. I was full of rage for the most trivial situations, got into the wrong relationships, and even stayed when I knew I should move on. My mental health hit the rocks and even though I expected people to understand, they just could not, and I had to accept that.

The only thing I "enjoyed" was work. I was fulfilled, working round the clock. I worked myself out so that I could get home exhausted and just sleep. I lost so much weight and became a downright shadow of myself.

I wanted to make sense of the loss because I felt his death had been unnecessary at the time. I continued to switch between different dysphoric emotions - becoming quickly irritated, angry at every little mistake and often overwhelmed with life as I could not initiate new friendships or maintain the ones I already had. Nothing else was important anymore as the most important person, the one whose validations mattered most was gone. I did not even see a reason to continue living as I started thinking of ways to disappear.

Someone once said, "The hardest part of losing someone is not having to say goodbye, but rather learning to live without them - always trying to fill the void, the emptiness that is left inside your heart when they go." And having to go through that seemingly familiar pain all over again just when you thought you were finally healing from one, can be overly distressing.

I was unable to sleep or cry, just dumbfounded,

yearning for healing. Grief can do that to you. It is like a rainy day, cold, cloudy, full of storms, slippery floors, leaking roofs, lacking warmth, snuggles, and sleep.

However, no matter how long it rains, one day, the sun will shine again, and hope will be restored.

LOVE LETTER

Dear Friend,

Life is about seasons. You must embrace the truth that all seasons are crucial to your purpose.

Leaving home to a far country, helped me cope with a tough season. It was not the best time to leave home, but it was part of the road map of my life. I saw my home and my life from a different view by myself and I appreciated everything about me and my home country correctly. Best of all, I experienced growth in isolation and did not even realize I was growing.

Summer sounds exciting but it does not mean that it will be so. Sometimes, your joy finally reaches you and you are not exactly relishing it as much as you expected. Don't beat yourself up. After all, everything it takes for you to be truly happy is already in you, so it is now up to you to bring yourself the summer you want with what you have been given. Lemonade did come from lemons remember.

If like me, you eventually live outside your home, you will come to realize that what you hear is different from what you see. Most times what you hear is exaggerated and sometimes, it is played down but be rest assured that what you see will enlighten you. Your mind will be opened, and you might get a chance to understand yourself more.

Your mindset will reorganize itself and at some point, no one will tell you to behave like a Roman when in Rome, it will just come naturally.

You will be tempted to change the way you speak but try to be original no matter how much they act like they do not understand you, they eventually will. That accent is part of your identity, don't lose it. When your people hear you, they will identify you and you might just get favors for it.

You will find out that a lot of people don't like Africans for several misjudged reasons, but they will not agree that it is coming from a place of envy and that is, unfortunately, their problem, not yours.

When you are away and you feel very sick, you will start to feel the need to see family. The symptoms include confusion, self-doubt, headache, stomach upset, flu, talking to yourself, loneliness, and whatever else you may feel. These all mean you are homesick, but you will be okay as soon as you treat symptoms and talk to your loved ones. If symptoms persist, make plans to visit home soonest.

Love might find you when you are not even expecting it, or you might just find it if you get desperate enough to look. Any which way, I believe love is sweeter when you are away from home. You are a lot more liberal with your decisions and more vulnerable but be careful because if it all goes wrong, you might end up with trust issues for a very long time. I am not sure there is a cure for that. However, your prayers will help if you stay consistent.

Get a job. Earn in the currency of the land you live in (if you must) so that you can afford the basic things of life. It will be sad for you to run out of savings especially if you have no support from anyone. Except you absolutely do not need to. Have something to offer, you can easily offer a service at a reduced fee. Do not be useless. Period.

Be kind to people. When they smile at you, smile in return. When they ask for the way, show them, when they push you over or try to cheat you, repay them with love, and most importantly, let go and forgive people that barely know you. There is no point fighting people on the bus, train, or anywhere. Chances are, you will get over whatever the issue is and may never see them again. So, again, be intentionally kind.

Do not make mistakes foolishly. When the people who have lived there longer than you warn you about something, please take their advice seriously. It could be about the weather, food, a certain behavior, a place, a shop, whatever it is, verify but believe them and learn.

You will get lost a few times. It is okay because you will eventually find your way. It is good to trust your instincts but don't do it all the time. Ask questions, even if they sound stupid, ask anyway.

Try different cuisines, don't crave your native cuisine all the time. Just try something that probably looks yuck and let your taste buds do the judgment. Food is a very easy way to deal with your social anxiety if you do have that.

Again, Summer is coming so be prepared to enjoy your joy in the best possible way.

Love always,

Busola

ABOUT THE AUTHOR

Oluwabusola Okewumi is a creative professional, born in the megacity of Lagos, Nigeria. Having lived without family in the UAE for a little over four years, she experienced isolation in a way that shaped her thoughts and view of life.

Growing up, she was fascinated by the art of storytelling, and writing a book was always top on her bucket list after she got a graduate degree in English Language. Eventually, with her stunning, debut memoir, Summer is Coming, it became a reality.

Busola considers her faith and family the most important to her. She can usually be found reading a book that will more likely than not be non-fiction. When not absorbed in the latest revealing page-turner, Busola loves to visit family, enjoys watching and listening to real-life stories, planning parties - and otherwise spends far too much time on the computer writing short stories.

To reach the author for more information and book orders:

Call:

+2348062240672

Email:

busolaokewumi@gmail.com

Printed in Great Britain
by Amazon